Changing
Stories

Acknowledgements

This book on fairy stories and folk tales was written and piloted during 1983-4 as part of an English Centre school focussed project on English and Gender.

We are grateful to authors and publishers, who have given permission to use their stories. We would be pleased to hear from any holders of copyright whom we have been unable to trace.

Fairy Stories and Folk Tales was compiled and written by Bronwyn Mellor with Judith Hemming and Jane Leggett.

'The Practical Princess' and 'Philbert the Fearful' from *The Practical Princess and Other Liberating Fairy Tales* by Jay Williams reprinted by permission of The Bodley Head. 'Mizilca' and 'Gone is Gone' from *Clever Gretchen' and Other Forgotten Folk Tales* retold by Alison Lurie, and 'Two Sisters and Two Bowls' from *The Story Spirits* by Amabel Williams Ellis reprinted by permission of William Heinemann Ltd. 'The Story of Grandmother' (Delarue), 'Little Red Riding Hood' (Charles Perrault) and 'Little Red Cap' (J & W Grimm) reprinted with permission from *Trials and Tribulations of Little Red Riding Hood* by Jack Zipes published in 1983 by Bergin and Garvey Publishers, USA. 'Red Riding Hood' from *Once and Future Tales* reprinted by permission of the Merseyside Fairy Story Collective. 'How Crab Got Its Back' from *Listen to this Story* by Grace Hallworth reprinted by permission of the author and Methuen Children's Books. 'Prince of Nettles' from *The Whole World Storybook* by Marcus Crouch, illustrated by William Stobbs (1983) reprinted by permission of Oxford University Press. 'The Man Who Knew Better' from *Folk Tales* by Leila Berg reprinted by permission of Hodder and Stoughton Children's Books. 'The Lute Player' copyright 1978 by Ethel Johnston Phelps from *Tatterhood and Other Tales* reprinted with permission of The Feminist Press, Box 334, Old Westbury, New York 11568. 'The Husband Who Stayed at Home' and 'Gawain and Lady Ragnell' copyright Ethel Johnston Phelps from *The Maid of the North* reprinted with permission of Holt Rinehart and Winston. 'The Little Girl and the Wolf' copyright 1940 James Thurber, copyright 1968 Helen Thurber from *Fables of Our Time* published by Harper and Row, reprinted with permission of Helen Thurber.

Published by The English & Media Centre, 18 Compton Terrace, London N1 2UN
Design: Daphne Denaro
Cover: Michael Foreman
Illustration: Jane Lydbury
© English & Media Centre, 1984
ISBN: 0907016 16 2

This Book Is About...

This book is about folk and fairy stories.

It is about who told the stories and who listened to them, and how the stories changed as they were retold by different tellers to different listeners.

It is about what happened when the stories came to be written down and collected into books: about the writers, the collectors and how the stories again changed as they were rewritten by different writers for different readers.

It is about what you have come to expect of folk and fairy stories, because you already know a lot about them; perhaps more than you realise.

When you were younger you enjoyed listening to and reading stories: now as well as reading for enjoyment you are able to explore the meanings and messages of stories and understand how and why they have changed over the years.

This is important because stories are one of the ways by which we are taught about the world we live in and how we are expected to behave in it as girls and boys, men and women.

Contents

At the back of this book are teachers' notes and suggested books for further reading.

1. WHAT YOU EXPECT...

The Practical Princess
Mizilca
Philbert the Fearful

Frogs, Princesses

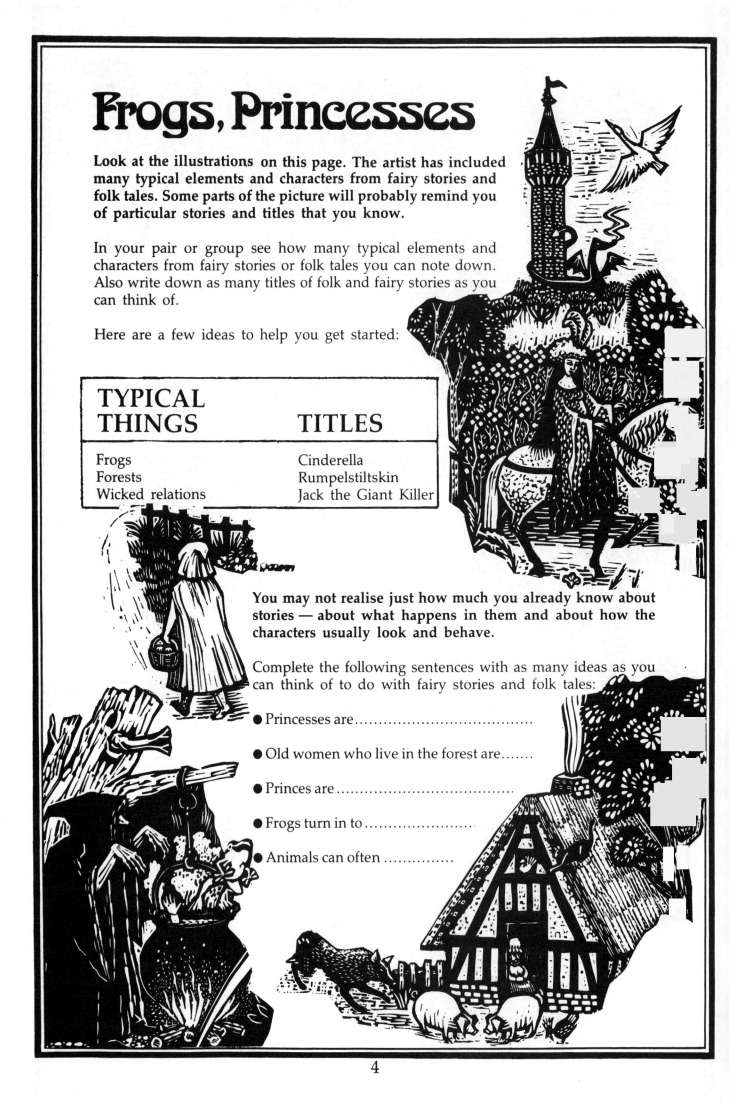

Look at the illustrations on this page. The artist has included many typical elements and characters from fairy stories and folk tales. Some parts of the picture will probably remind you of particular stories and titles that you know.

In your pair or group see how many typical elements and characters from fairy stories or folk tales you can note down. Also write down as many titles of folk and fairy stories as you can think of.

Here are a few ideas to help you get started:

TYPICAL THINGS	TITLES
Frogs	Cinderella
Forests	Rumpelstiltskin
Wicked relations	Jack the Giant Killer

You may not realise just how much you already know about stories — about what happens in them and about how the characters usually look and behave.

Complete the following sentences with as many ideas as you can think of to do with fairy stories and folk tales:

● Princesses are......................................

● Old women who live in the forest are.......

● Princes are.......................................

● Frogs turn in to.........................

● Animals can often ....

The Princess

You are going to read a story about a princess called Bedelia. But before you read it, see if you can work out how the story will go.

These are the main events:

(1) **Bedelia is given three gifts by fairies when she is born.**

What are they?

(2) **A dragon comes into the neighbour-hood when Bedelia is eighteen.**

What does the dragon want?

(3) **The dragon is killed.**

Who kills it, and how?

(4) **An old, greedy lord called Garp wants to marry Bedelia.**

What does Bedelia think? What does her father think?

(5) **Bedelia is imprisoned in a tower.**

Who by? Why?

(6) **Bedelia meets a young prince called Perian.**

What is he like?

(7) **Bedelia escapes from the tower.**

How?

(8) **Lord Garp is killed.**

Who by and how?

(9) **There is a ceremony at the end of the story.**

What is it? Who is taking part?

The Practical Princess

Princess Bedelia was as lovely as the moon shining upon a lake full of waterlilies. She was as graceful as a cat leaping. And she was also extremely practical.

When she was born, three fairies had come to her cradle to give her gifts as was usual in that country. The first fairy had given her beauty. The second had given her grace. But the third, who was a wise old creature, had said, "I give her common sense."

"I don't think much of that gift," said King Ludwig, raising his eyebrows. "What good is common sense to a princess? All she needs is charm."

Nevertheless, when Bedelia was eighteen years old, something happened which made the king change his mind.

A dragon moved into the neighbourhood. He settled in a dark cave on top of a mountain, and the first thing he did was to send a message to the king. "I must have a princess to devour," the message said, "Or I shall breathe out my fiery breath and destroy the kingdom."

Sadly, King Ludwig called together his councillors and read them the message. "Perhaps," said the Prime Minister, "we had better advertise for a knight to slay the dragon? That is what is generally done in these cases."

"I'm afraid we haven't time," answered the king. "The dragon has only given us until tomorrow morning. There is no help for it. We shall have to send him the princess." Princess Bedelia had come to the meeting because, as she said, she liked to mind her own business and this was certainly her business.

"Rubbish!" she said. "Dragons can't tell the difference between princesses and anyone else. Use your common sense. He's just asking for me because he's a snob."

"That may be so," said her father, "but if we don't send you along, he'll destroy the kingdom."

"Right!" said Bedelia. "I see I'll have to deal with this myself." She left the council chamber. She got the largest and gaudiest of her state robes and stuffed it with straw, and tied it together with string. Into the centre of the bundle she packed about a hundred pounds of gunpowder. She got two strong young men to carry it up the mountain for her. She stood in front of the dragon's cave, and called, "Come out! Here's the princess!"

The dragon came blinking and peering out of the darkness. Seeing the bright robe covered with gold and silver embroidery, and hearing Bedelia's voice, he opened his mouth wide.

At Bedelia's signal, the two young men swung the robe and gave it a good heave, right down the dragon's throat. Bedelia threw herself flat on the ground, and the two young men ran.

As the gunpowder met the flames inside the dragon, there was a tremendous explosion.

Bedelia got up, dusting herself off. "Dragons," she said, "are not very bright."

She left the two young men sweeping up the pieces, and she went back to the castle to have her geography lesson.

The lesson that morning was local geography. "Our kingdom, Arapathia, is bounded on the north by Istven," said the teacher. "Lord Garp, the ruler of Istven, is old, rich and greedy." At that very moment, Lord Garp of Istven was arriving at the castle. Word of Bedelia's destruction of the dragon had reached him. "That girl," said he, "is just the wife for me." And he had come with a hundred finely-dressed courtiers and many presents to ask King Ludwig for her hand.

The king sent for Bedelia. "My dear," he said, clearing his throat nervously, "just see who is here."

"I see. It's Lord Garp." said Bedelia. She turned to go.

"He wants to marry you," said the king.

Bedelia looked at Lord Garp. His face was like an old napkin, crumpled and wrinkled. It was covered with warts, as if someone had left crumbs on the napkin. He had only two teeth. Six long hairs grew from his chin, and none on his head. She felt like screaming.

However, she said, "I'm very flattered. Thank you, Lord Garp. Just let me talk to my father in private for a minute." When they had retired to a small room behind the throne, Bedelia said to the king, "What will Lord Garp do if I refuse to marry him?"

"He is rich, greedy, and crafty," said the king unhappily. "He is also used to having his own way in everything. He will be insulted. He will probably declare war on us, and then there will be trouble."

"Very well," said Bedelia. "We must be practical."

She returned to the throne room. Smiling sweetly at Lord Garp, she said, "My lord, as you know, it is customary for a princess to set tasks for anyone who wishes to marry her. Surely you wouldn't like me to break the custom. And you are bold and powerful enough, I know, to perform any task."

"That is true," said Lord Garp smugly, stroking the six hairs on his chin. "Name your task."

"Bring me," said Bedelia, "a branch from the Jewel Tree of Paxis."

Lord Garp bowed, and off he went. "I think," said Bedelia to her father, "that we have seen the last of him. For Paxis is a thousand miles away, and the Jewel Tree is guarded by lions, serpents and wolves."

But in two weeks, Lord Garp was back. With him he bore a chest, and from the chest he took a wonderful twig. Its bark was of rough gold. The leaves that grew from it were of fine silver. The twig was covered with blossoms, and each blossom had petals of mother-of-pearl and centres of sapphires, the colour of the evening sky.

Bedelia's heart sank as she took the twig. But then she said to herself, "Use your common sense, my girl! Lord Garp never travelled two thousand miles in two weeks, nor is he the man to fight his way through lions, serpents and wolves."

She looked more carefully at the branch. Then she said, "My lord, you know that the Jewel Tree of Paxis is a living tree, although it is all made of jewels."

"Why, of course," said Lord Garp. "Everyone knows that."

"Well," said Bedelia, "then why is it that these blossoms have no scent?"

Lord Garp turned red.

"I think," Bedelia went on, "that this branch was made by the jewellers of Istven, who are the best in the world. Not very nice of you, my lord. Some people might even call it cheating."

Lord Garp shrugged. He was too old and rich to feel ashamed. But like many men used to having their own way, the more Bedelia refused him, the more he was determined to have her.

"Never mind all that," he said. "Set me another task. This time, I swear I will perform it."

Bedelia sighed. "Very well. Then bring me a cloak made from the skins of the salamanders who live in the Volcano of Scoria."

Lord Garp bowed, and off he went. "The Volcano of Scoria," said Bedelia to her father, "is covered with red-hot lava. It burns steadily with great flames, and pours out poisonous smoke so that no one can come within a mile of it."

"You have certainly profited by your geography lessons," said the king, with admiration.

Nevertheless, in a week, Lord Garp was back. This time, he carried a cloak that shone and rippled like all the colours of fire. It was made of scaly skins, stitched together with golden wire as fine as a hair, and each scale was red and orange and blue, like a tiny flame.

Bedelia took the splendid cloak. She said to herself. "Use your head, miss! Lord Garp never climbed the red-hot slopes of the Volcano of Scoria."

A fire was burning in the fireplace of the throne room. Bedelia hurled the cloak into it. The skins blazed up in a flash, blackened, and fell to ashes.

Lord Garp turned pale with anger. He hopped up and down, unable at first to do anything but splutter.

"Ub-ub-ub!" he cried. Then, controlling himself, he said, "So be it. If I can't have you, no one shall!"

He pointed a long, skinny finger at her. On the finger was a magic ring. At once, a great wind arose. It blew through the throne room. It sent King Ludwig flying one way and his guards the other. It picked up Bedelia and whisked her off through the air. When she could catch her breath and look about her, she found herself in a room at the top of a tower.

Bedelia peered out of the window. About the tower stretched an empty, barren plain. As she watched, a speck appeared in the distance. A plume of dust rose behind it. It drew nearer and became Lord Garp on horseback.

He rode to the tower and looked up at Bedelia. "Aha!" he croaked. "So you are safe and snug, are you? And will you marry me now?"

"Never," said Bedelia, firmly.

"Then stay there until never comes," snarled Lord Garp.

Away he rode.

For the next two days, Bedelia felt very sorry for herself. She sat wistfully by the window, looking out at the empty plain. When she was hungry, food appeared on the table. When she was tired, she lay down on the narrow cot and slept. Each day, Lord Garp rode by and asked her if she had changed her mind, and each day she refused him. Her only hope was that, as so often happens in old tales, a prince might come riding by who would rescue her.

But on the third day, she gave herself a shake.

"Now, then, pull yourself together," she said sternly. "If you sit waiting for a prince to rescue you, you may sit here forever. Be practical! If there's any rescuing to be done, you're going to have to do it yourself."

She jumped up. There was something she had not yet done, and now she did it. She tried the door.

It opened.

Outside, were three other doors. But there was no sign of a stair, or any way down from the top of the tower.

She opened two of the doors and found that they led into cells just like hers, but empty.

Behind the fourth door, however, lay what appeared to be a haystack.

From beneath it came the sound of snores. And between snores, a voice said, "Sixteen million and twelve . . . *snore* . . . sixteen million and thirteen . . . *snore* . . . sixteen million and fourteen . . ."

Cautiously, she went closer. Then she saw what she had taken for a haystack was in fact an immense pile of blond hair. Parting it, she found a young man, fast asleep.

As she stared, he opened his eyes. He blinked at her. "Who—?" he said. Then he said, "Sixteen million and fifteen," closed his eyes, and fell asleep again.

Bedelia took him by the shoulder and shook him hard. He awoke, yawning, and tried to sit up. But the mass of hair made this difficult.

"What on earth is the matter with you?" Bedelia asked. "Who are you?"

"I am Prince Perian," he replied, "the rightful ruler of— oh, dear, here I go again. Sixteen million and. . ." His eyes began to close.

Bedelia shook him again. He made a violent effort and managed to wake up enough to continue, "—of Istven. But Lord Garp has put me under a spell. I have to count sheep jumping over a fence, and this puts me to slee-ee-ee-."

He began to snore lightly.

"Dear me," said Bedelia. "I must do something."

She thought hard. Then she pinched Perian's ear, and this woke him with a start. "Listen," she said. "It's quite simple. It's all in your mind, you see. You are imagining the sheep jumping over the fence —No! Don't go to sleep again!"

"This is what you must do. Imagine them jumping backwards. As you do, *count* them backwards and when you get to *one*, you'll be wide awake."

The prince's eyes snapped open. "Marvellous!" he said. "Will it work?"

"It's bound to," said Bedelia. "For if the sheep going one way will put you to sleep, their going back again will wake you up."

Hastily, the prince began to count, "Six million and fourteen, six million and thirteen, six million and twelve . . ."

"Oh, my goodness," cried Bedelia, "count by hundreds, or you'll never get there."

He began to gabble as fast as he could, and with each moment that passed, his eyes sparkled more brightly, his face grew livelier, and he seemed a little stronger, until at last, he shouted, "Five, four, three two, ONE!" and awoke completely.

He struggled to his feet, with a little help from Bedelia.

"Heavens!" he said. "Look how my fair and beard have grown. I've been here for years. Thank you, my dear. Who are you, and what are you doing here?"

Bedelia quickly explained.

Perian shook his head. "One more crime of Lord Garp's," he said. "We must escape and see that he is punished."

"Easier said than done," Bedelia replied. "There is no stair in this tower, as far as I can tell, and the outside wall is much too smooth to climb."

Perian frowned. "This will take some thought," he said. "What we need is a long rope."

"Use your common sense," said Bedelia. "We haven't any rope."

Then her face brightened, and she clapped her hands. "But we have your beard," she laughed.

Perian understood at once, and chuckled. "I'm sure it will reach almost to the ground," he said. "But we haven't any scissors to cut it off with."

"That is so," said Bedelia. "Hang it out of the window and let me climb down. I'll search the tower and perhaps I can find a ladder, or a hidden stair. If all else fails, I can go for help."

She and the prince gathered up great armfuls of the beard and staggered into Bedelia's room, which had the largest window. The prince's long hair trailed behind him and nearly tripped him.

He threw the beard out of the window, and sure enough the end of it came to within a few feet of the ground.

Perian braced himself, holding the beard with both hands to ease the pull on his chin. Bedelia climbed out of the window and slid down the beard. She dropped to the ground and sat for a moment, breathless.

And as she sat there, out of the wilderness came the drumming of hooves, a cloud of dust, and then Lord Garp on his swift horse.

With one glance, he saw what was happening. He shook his fist up at Prince Perian.

"Meddlesome fool!" he shouted. "I'll teach you to interfere."

He leapt from the horse and grabbed the beard. He gave it a tremendous yank. Headfirst came Perian, out of the window. Down he fell, and with a thump, he landed right on top of old Lord Garp.

This saved Perian, who was not hurt at all. But it was the end of Lord Garp.

Perian and Bedelia rode back to Istven on Lord Garp's horse.

In the great city, the prince was greeted with cheers of joy — once everyone recognised him after so many years and under so much hair.

And of course, since Bedelia had rescued him from captivity, she married him. First, however, she made him get a haircut and a shave so that she could see what he really looked like.

For she was always practical.

The Practical Princess

In each box below there is a sentence describing an event or character in a fairy story. Some of the sentences are about events and characters that are typical or usual in fairy stories. But some of the sentences are about things which aren't usual in fairy stories.

They show how the writer of *The Practical Princess* **changed the usual events and characters which we have come to expect in fairy stories.**

Read through all the sentences in the boxes. Decide which ones you would put under each heading on the chart that follows.

A A dragon comes to the kingdom wanting to eat a princess, who blows it up with dynamite.

I There is a new-born princess, who is given three presents by good fairies: beauty, grace and commonsense.

B The villain is killed by the prince in a sword fight.

J There is a sleepy prince.

C The princess rescues the prince.

K The princess's suitor performs the tasks set for him by the princess by cheating.

D There is a new-born princess, who is given three presents by good fairies: beauty, grace and a sweet temper.

L The villain is killed by the prince, who falls out of a window on top of him.

E There is a handsome prince.

M The prince and princess marry and live happily ever after.

F The princess is locked up in a tower, where she decides she must work out for herself how to escape.

N A dragon comes to the kingdom wanting to eat a princess, and is killed by a prince with a lance.

G The prince rescues the princess.

O The prince and princess marry after the princess has decided for herself that the prince is suitable.

H The princess's suitor succeeds in doing the tasks set for him by the princess's father.

P The princess is locked up in a tower, where she waits for a brave and handsome prince to rescue her.

The Practical Princess

Write down the letters matching the sentences in the boxes on the last page under the heading USUAL or UNUSUAL, on a chart like the one below. For example:

USUAL	UNUSUAL
M The prince and princess marry and live happily ever after.	**O** The prince and princess marry after the princess has decided for herself that the prince is suitable.

Why did the writer write the story in this way?

Pick two or three of the statements below which you think might best explain why the writer made *The Practical Princess* different from the usual fairy story.

1. The writer wanted to make the readers laugh.

2. The writer was bored with the usual fairy stories and felt like a change.

3. The writer wanted to write a modern story.

4. The writer wanted to make the readers think about what usually happens in fairy stories.

5. The writer wanted to show that girls in stories can be confident and clever.

6. The writer didn't know how to write a proper fairy story.

7. The writer wanted to show that boys in stories can be gentle.

Mizilca & Philbert

You know a lot about what usually happens in fairy stories and folk tales. You also know a lot about the characters in these stories — what they usually look like, how they usually behave and what they usually do.

From just this picture you can probably predict quite a lot about the character on the horse, and how the usual story involving such a character would go.

Mizilca & Philbert

BEFORE READING

You are going to read two stories. One has a young heroine (woman) called Mizilca; the other has a young hero (man) called Philbert.

From your knowledge of typical fairy stories or folk tales what would you expect **Mizilca** (the heroine) and **Philbert** (the hero) are going to be like?

Write the sentences that you would expect to be true of Mizilca and Philbert, if they were the usual kind of heroine and hero, on to your copy of the chart under the heading EXPECTATIONS.

(You'll fill in the other columns after you have read the stories.)

— to be weak and afraid

— to be a fearless knight

— to like adventures

— to be able to fight fiercely

— to like beautiful silk materials and jewels

— to like to stay at home quietly

— to enjoy excitement and action

— to look beautiful

— to think personal appearance is very important

— to fight battles

CHARACTERS	Mizilca	Philbert
EXPECTATIONS What we expect the characters to be like:		
BEHAVIOUR What the characters are like in the stories:		
QUALITIES What qualities the characters show:		

Mizilca

L ong ago and far away, there lived a knight who was skilled in magic. One day a messenger came to him from the Sultan, demanding that the knight come with horse and arms, or send one of his sons, to serve the Sultan for a year and a day. The knight did not know what to do, for he was old and lame, and had no sons, only three daughters. So troubled was he that he ceased to take any joy in living. At home and abroad he was continually downcast, and whenever he looked at his children he would sigh and shake his head.

At last his eldest daughter, whose name was Stanuta, said to him, "Dear father, what ails you? Have we done something to displease you?"

"No, my child," said the knight. "I am sighing because the Sultan has commanded me to send a knight to serve at his court for a year and a day. If I cannot do so, I am dishonoured; yet I am old and have no sons."

"I am strong and healthy," said Stanuta. "Change me into a young man by your magic arts, and I shall go to the Sultan."

"Alas," answered her father, "my skill does not go so far."

"Then I will tell you what you must do," said Stanuta. "Give me a horse and arms; let my hair be cut like a man's and I shall go."

At first the old knight protested, but presently he agreed to his daughter's plan. Stanuta had her long hair cut off, and her father gave her one of the finest horses in his stable, and the best of weapons and armour. But on the morning she was to start for the Sultan's palace, the old knight rode out ahead of her secretly until he came to a bridge at the boundary of his lands. There he changed himself into the likeness of a blue boar, and hid in the woods beside the river.

When Stanuta reached the bridge, the seeming boar charged out, snorting and pawing the ground. She screamed with terror, turned her horse's head around, and galloped back to the castle.

Next the knight's second daughter, whose name was Roxanda, asked for arms and a horse, so that she might go to the Sultan and serve him in her father's place. She swore that she would ride straight to the palace, and that no boar would turn her from her path. So her father gave her a good horse, and well-made weapons and armour, and Roxanda had her hair cut like a man's. On the day she was to set out, the old knight went ahead of her as before to the river, changed himself into the likeness of a red lion, and hid among the trees.

When Roxanda came to the bridge, the seeming lion leapt out at her, roaring and lashing its tail. She was struck so dumb with fright that she could not utter a word. Shaking like a poplar tree in the wind, she turned her horse and galloped home to the castle.

Now the knight's youngest daughter, who was called Mizilca, asked that she might have a horse and arms, and she would have her hair cut off and go to the Sultan. But her father refused, saying, "My dear daughter, how can you hope to succeed where your sisters, who are older and stronger than you, have failed? Stay home, and keep your long hair." Mizilca would not listen to him, but kept begging to go, saying no boar or lion would stand in her way. At last, to be rid of her pleading, her father gave her a rusty sword and lance, and allowed her to saddle an old grey horse that had done nothing for years but pull the cart. On the morning she was to set out, he left the castle before her, took on the likeness of a green dragon, and concealed himself in the trees by the river.

When Mizilca came to the bridge, the dragon rushed out at her, breathing smoke and fire. Mizilca did not falter, but put spurs to her horse and galloped at him; and the seeming dragon had to run away into the woods to escape being pierced by a real lance. Mizilca did not pursue him, but crossed the bridge and rode on.

Arriving at the palace, Mizilca went before the Sultan, bowed low, and told him that she was the old knight's son, come to serve him for a year and a day. The Sultan looked her up and down, and thought to himself that this was no youth at all, but a maiden. Yet

Mizilca stood so straight and spoke out so boldly that he doubted his own eyes. So he welcomed her and admitted her into his company of knights.

The weeks passed, and the Sultan saw that Mizilca could ride and fight and shoot with bow and arrows as well as any of his knights. Yet still, whenever he looked at her, he suspected that she was no man. At last he went to a wise-woman and asked how he could discover whether Mizilca was a youth or a maiden. The wise-woman advised him to have merchants come to the palace while Mizilca was out hunting, and place on one side of the great hall rich cloths and embroideries of silk and velvet, and on the other side all kinds of swords and daggers. "If the knight is a maiden," said the wise-woman, "she will be drawn to the cloths, and pay no heed to the weapons."

And so it was done. But when Mizilca came into the hall and saw the goods laid out, she suspected that the Sultan was testing her. She ignored the silks and velvets and went straight to the weapons, feeling the edges of the blades and making passes with the swords in the air as if fighting.

Time went on, and though Mizilca continued to excel at all knightly pursuits, the Sultan was still not satisfied that she was a man. He went again to the wise-woman, and she advised him to have his cook prepare kasha for dinner, and mix a spoonful of pearls into Mizilca's portion. "If the knight is a maiden," said she, "she will pick out the pearls and save them."

And so it was done. But again Mizilca was too clever for the Sultan. She took the pearls out of the kasha and cast them under the table as if they had been pebbles.

At last the year and a day had passed, and it was time for Mizilca to return home. The Sultan came out to bid her farewell, and said to her, "Mizilca, you have served me well, and paid the debt your father owed. Before you go, answer me one question. Are you a youth or a maiden?" Mizilca did not answer him, but mounted her horse and rode out through the palace gate. Then she turned and opened wide her shirt so that all could see she was a woman, calling out:

High and mighty Sultan praised be,
Though your word is law o'er land and sea,
I know more of you than you of me.

Then she spurred her horse, and rode off towards her father's castle, where she was welcomed with much joy and feasting.

Philbert The Fearful

Sir Philbert Fitzhugh was not very brave. This wouldn't have mattered had he been a merchant or a mason or a mouse-catcher, but he was a knight. Other knights went riding out to slay dragons or rescue princesses, but Sir Philbert stayed comfortably at home taking care of his health, curled up by the fire with a good book and an apple.

"After all," he said, "I am the only one of me I have, and I have to take care of myself."

Everyone said, "Knights ought to be brave as lions."

"Maybe so," replied Sir Philbert. "But *I* think it's more important to keep your health." And he went back to his reading and his fire and his apple. "An apple a day," he added, "keeps the doctor away."

Nevertheless, the doctor came one day and had dinner, and he poked Sir Philbert in the chest and looked at his tongue and felt his pulse. Then he shook his head.

"You're getting flabby," he said sternly. "Look at yourself! You're pale. You've got the beginnings of a pot-belly. I recommend a long trip and a change of scene."

"But I get homesick," Sir Philbert protested.

The doctor snorted. "Fiddlesticks! Tomorrow morning," said he, "three bold knights are going to search for the emperor's daughter, who has been kidnapped by an enchanter named Brasilgore. I order you to go with them. The adventure will be the best thing for you."

The next morning at half-past four, the three bold knights started out on their quest. With them was a fourth knight, not so bold. It was Sir Philbert.

He had plenty of warm blankets rolled up behind his saddle. He had plenty of food and medicine in his saddlebags. But he was far from happy.

The other three knights, however, were perfectly happy. They were named Sir Hugo of Brandish, Sir Armet of Anguish, and Sir Brian of Thump. Their armour was rusty and dented from many adventures. In their saddlebags they carried nothing but bread and hard cheese. Their moustaches were as fierce as their talk.

"We'll slay Brasilgore the enchanter, and find the emperor's daughter, or die in the attempt!" roared Sir Brian.

"Then I certainly hope we find her," mumbled Sir Philbert.

They travelled for many days until they came to a wide, sad plain. Nothing grew there but twisted thorn bushes and purple heather. A wind from the north blew steadily over it. They rode and rode through the heather and into the wind, and at noon they came to a tower. It was high and black. It had one window at the top and a door in front which was a good deal higher than a house.

As they gazed up at it, wondering what it was for, a maiden put her head out of the window.

"Help, help", she cried.

Sir Brian shaded his eyes. "Are you a prisoner?" he called.

"Yes, I am. Please go away," said the maiden.

"Eh?" Sir Brian looked puzzled. "But you just said, "Help, help."

"Oh, dear, I know I did. I'm sorry. I said 'Help, help', but I meant go away."

"But why?" asked Sir Hugo of Brandish.

Just then the enormous door opened. "That's why," said the maiden. "Alas, alas, this is the end of you. Goodbye."

Out stepped a giant a good deal higher than a house. He drew a deep breath, stretched and yawned. It sounded like a thunderstorm overhead.

Sir Hugo lowered his lance. "Stand back, all of you," he shouted. "This giant is mine!".

He rode straight at the giant's ankle and thrust his lance.

"Oh, well done," said Sir Brian.

The giant uttered a yell, "Hornets!" He stamped his foot angrily. Sir Hugo disappeared.

"Adventures!" groaned Sir Philbert. "I just wish that rotten doctor were here."

The other two knights stared uneasily at each other and then at the giant who was grumbling like an earthquake.

Sir Philbert quickly unfastened his big roll of blankets. He shook them out. He turned his horse and began to gallop away. Letting the blankets stream behind him like banners.

The giant saw Sir Philbert and made a giant stride to mash him. Sir Philbert let go of the blankets. They blew away in the endless wind. They flew up and plastered themselves over the giant's eyes. He missed his footing, stumbled on a rock, and fell on his head with a crash. Since he was so much bigger and heavier than an ordinary person, he fell with a far bigger and heavier crash. It was the end of him.

Sir Armet and Sir Brian trotted over and stared at the giant's body. They shook their heads.

"Listen," said Sir Armet, "I don't think that was very sporting."

"It was nothing but an accident," Sir Brian agreed. "Philbert didn't kill the giant. He killed himself."

"Yes, I suppose he did," said Sir Philbert. He opened his helmet and mopped his forehead. "But I came on this quest for my health, you know. It wouldn't have been very healthy to go the way poor Hugo went, now would it?"

The maiden came running out of the tower. Sir Philbert took off his helmet, for he was always very polite.

"I'm glad to say you are no longer a prisoner, Miss," he said.

"Oh, thank you," smiled the maiden, who had large, merry brown eyes and long brown hair in two braids down her back. "I'll just get my things, if you'll wait a minute."

"What?" huffed Sir Brian. "Get your things?".

"Of course. I'm coming with you. You rescued me, didn't you?"

"You can't come with us," said Sir Armet. "It's much too dangerous."

"Besides, we haven't an extra horse," said Sir Brian.

"She can ride with me," Sir Philbert said.

The maiden smiled at him. She ran into the tower and soon returned with four large bundles. They hung the bundles on Sir Philbert's horse, and Sir Philbert said it was just as well his blankets had all blown away. Then the maiden — whose name was Victoria — got up behind, and away they rode once more.

Victoria said, "I was watching from the window. Did you really expect those blankets to fly up over the giant's face?"

Sir Philbert sighed. "I hoped so," he said.

"If they hadn't, what would you have done?"

"I would have kept on riding as fast as I could. I didn't see how else I could beat a giant that tall."

"But shouldn't a knight be brave?"

"Oh, yes," said Sir Philbert. "But on the other hand, I'm the only one of me I have, and I have to take care of myself."

Victoria nodded. "That's reasonable," she said.

They rode on. At last they came to a high place. The road ran over a peak that sparkled with glassy ice. On each side, the rock fell away in steep cliffs, down, down, to glittering rock below. Sir Brian's horse suddenly reared and skittered round. Sir Armet's horse reared too. After a bit Sir Philbert and Victoria caught up with them and saw what they saw. Their horse couldn't rear because it was too heavily loaded.

There was a cockatrice in the way. It had the body of a serpent and the head and legs of a rooster. Its scales were green and shiny in the icy light. Its long serpent tongue flicked in and out of its cock's beak, and its round, evil eyes rolled forward to look at them. It strutted as tall as a man.

"Hmm," said Sir Philbert. "It might be better to go back and find another way. After all, we have a lady with us."

"Pah! You are a coward, sir," said Sir Armet. "Stand back, all of you."

He lowered his lance and galloped forward.

"Oh, dear," Sir Philbert whispered to Victoria.

Sir Armet's lance shattered on the green scales. The cockatrice hissed. It darted its rooster's beak forward on its snaky neck. Sir Armet's horse gave a scream and plunged over the edge of the cliff with Sir Armet.

"Stand back, all of you," said Sir Brian nervously. He began to lower his lance. But Sir Philbert caught his elbow.

"Wait a minute," said Sir Philbert. "I just thought of something I'd like to try."

He got off his horse. "Victoria, my dear," he said, "have you a mirror?"

"Oh, yes," she answered. She opened one of her bundles and took out a large, golden looking glass with her initial 'V' in emeralds on the back.

Sir Philbert took it and walked forward, his armour squeaking and clinking in the still, cold air. The cockatrice shot out its fearsome head once again. Sir Philbert held out the mirror.

The cockatrice stared into it. Then it gave a dithering hiss of horror, spread its wings, and flew away over the peaks.

Sir Philbert returned the looking glass to Victoria. He was shaking like a leaf.

"Why, how brave of you!" cried Victoria, giving him a hug.

"No, not very brave," said Sir Philbert. "The only thing a cockatrice is afraid of is another cockatrice. I was pretty sure it would fly off when it saw its face in the mirror. I read that in a book," he added humbly.

"Then it was very clever of you," Victoria said firmly.

"Hmph!" grunted Sir Brian. "Clever? I'm not so sure a knight *ought* to be clever."

Sir Philbert hung his head. "I know. But you see, I'm the only one of me I have. . ."

"Suppose we have a bite of lunch and then push on," Sir Brian said briskly.

When they had finished eating, they followed the road over the top of the mountain and down the other side. After a time, Sir Philbert remarked, "These trees are growing in rows, almost like a park."

"Rubbish!" said Sir Brian. "It's a wild wood."

"There's no underbrush either," Sir Philbert continued.

"Ridiculous!" said Sir Brian. "Next you'll be telling me you see a castle."

"I see a castle," Sir Philbert said.

Sure enough, the trees ended at a bridge, and on the other side of it there was a gloomy castle with many turrets.

"Ha!" Sir Brian exclaimed. "The castle of the enchanter!"

"Are you sure?" asked Sir Philbert.

"Of course I'm sure. Don't you think I know what an enchanter's castle looks like?" Sir Brian retorted.

They rode across the bridge and under a gateway like a giant's yawn, into a paved courtyard. All was silent.

Sir Brian rubbed his hands together. "Now then," he said, "the enchanter is probably upstairs in his den. I'll go after him. If anything happens to me — which isn't very likely because I know how to handle these fellows — just remember one rule. You must hold on to the enchanter until he surrenders. He will turn himself into all sorts of beasts: a lion, a wolf, a dragon, anything. As long as you hold him you're safe. If you let go of him, he'll magic you, and — *poof*!"

Sir Philbert nodded. "I've read all about that in. . ." he began, but Sir Brian was gone.

Sir Philbert rubbed his chin. "You know," he said to Victoria, "I'm not at all sure this is the right castle."

"Never mind," said Victoria.

"But I *do* mind. I think I'd better follow Brian. Suppose something happens to him."

"Suppose something happens to you?" said Victoria.

"Don't let's talk about it," Sir Philbert gulped.

He walked into the castle. There was a large cob-webby hall with a winding, dusty stair at one end of it. He could see Sir Brian's footprints in the dust. He began to follow them.

Now Sir Brian had climbed the stairs, and he had found, at the top, a heavy door opening into a tower room. Inside, there was a little old man with a bristle of untidy hair. Sir Brian sprang in and seized him by the neck.

"Ha, foul wizard," shouted Sir Brian, "I have thee!"

The old man at once turned into a lion. Sir Brian held fast. The lion became a fanged wolf. Sir Brian with a laugh still held him. The wolf became a dragon. Sir Brian held on. The dragon, in the blink of an eye, turned into a lady.

"Oh, you're hurting me," said the lady. "Not very knightly of you."

"I beg your pardon," said Sir Brian. He let go at once. The enchanter promptly waved his hand and turned Sir Brian into a pelican, which gave a dismal squawk and flew out of the window.

The enchanter changed back into himself and began to dust off his cloak. At that instant, Sir Philbert, who had seen the whole thing from the doorway, rushed in and grabbed the enchanter by the neck.

"What? Another one?" shrieked the enchanter.

He was so confused that he turned himself into a dreadful combination of lion, wolf, dragon, and woman all at once. Sir Philbert gritted his teeth and hung on. The enchanter then turned into a unicorn, a falcon, a salmon, a chest of drawers, a saber-toothed tiger, and a burning wastepaper basket. Sir Philbert held on for dear life. At last, the enchanter turned into a wasp. This time, Sir Philbert almost did let go. But he thought of his health and of Victoria and of poor blustering Sir Brian, who was now a pelican, and he gripped the wasp tightly. It didn't sting him after all. Instead, it turned back into the enchanter, looking extremely sulky.

"Very well," he panted. "You've won. What is your wish?"

"I want you to take the spell off Sir Brian," said Sir Philbert.

"What, right now?"

"At once."

The enchanter chuckled disagreeably. "Very well," he said. He waved his hand. Sir Brian, who was at that moment flying low over a swamp, changed back into himself and fell plop! into the mud.

"Anything else?" said the enchanter.

"Yes," said Sir Philbert, remembering the reason for the quest. "I want you to let the emperor's daughter go."

"Let her go? How can I let her go when I haven't got her?"

"Oh my," groaned Sir Philbert. "I knew it was the wrong castle. Well, who did kidnap her?"

"She was kidnapped by Brasilgore," said the enchanter. "And she has already been rescued."

"She has? Where is she?"

"Downstairs in my courtyard," snarled the enchanter. "Now, if there's nothing else I can do for you, will you please go away?"

But Sir Philbert had already gone, down the stairs two at a time.

"And so Brasilgore the enchanter was a giant," he said as he and Victoria went trotting off together, she riding more comfortably on Sir Brian's horse. "But why didn't you tell us?"

"You never asked me," Victoria replied.

"That's true. Well, I suppose I'd better take you home to your father as quickly as possible."

They travelled until they came to the emperor's empire. They entered the great city, and all the people ran out to cheer and stare and point. They came to the castle, and there was the emperor on a throne of ivory and emeralds. There was also Sir Brian, looking very muddy and rusty and bothered.

"Victoria, my darling, I'm so glad to see you again," said the emperor, embracing her. "Sir Brian was telling me how he had failed to find you."

Victoria hugged her father. "I must just tell you everything that has happened," she cried. And so she did.

When she had finished, the emperor said, "I have sworn to give half my kingdom and my daughter's hand to the man brave enough to rescue her."

Sir Philbert blushed. "My lord," he said, "I really don't want half your kingdom. I have a nice little castle of my own, and it's all I can do to manage it — but I *would* rather like to have Victoria."

Victoria smiled and took his hand.

Then Sir Brian interrupted. "My lord emperor," he cried, "that man didn't rescue your daughter by bravery. He killed the giant by accident and the cockatrice by a trick."

"Dear me," said the emperor. He stroked his beard thoughtfully. "Now let me get this straight. Where is Sir Hugo of Brandish?"

"He died a hero's death, sir," said Sir Brian.

"I see. And Sir Armet of Anguish?"

"Perished bravely in combat."

"Ah. And as for you, you'd still be a pelican if it hadn't been for Sir Philbert, eh?"

Sir Brian frowned. "But he is a coward!" he said.

"Ah, yes, there's that." The emperor turned to one of his servants and whispered in his ear. The servant turned pale and ran off. He came back in a few moments with a large box. From the box came a loud and angry humming.

"Now, gallant sirs," said the emperor, "here is a box containing a wasps' nest. I'd like one of you to reach inside and catch a wasp for me. There is no reward. I just want a wasp."

Sir Brian reached out a hand, listened to the furious humming, winced, and drew it back. Nobody else moved.

"You see," said the emperor, "when Sir Philbert held on to the enchanter he was being quite as brave as was necessary. Sir Philbert, will you reach in and get me a wasp?"

Sir Philbert swallowed hard. He had had more practice than anyone else, so to speak, but he didn't much want to do it again. Then, suddenly, he had an idea. He grinned. He pulled on one of his iron gloves, reached into the box, and took out a wasp.

Victoria laughed. She said to her father, "He's the only one of him there is, and I'm the only one of me there is, and he knows how to take care of both of us."

"Quite right," said the emperor. "I'd much rather have my daughter married to someone with sense enough to stay alive and take care of her than have her married to a pelican."

So Philbert and Victoria were married and rode happily home to take care of each other.

Mizilca & Philbert

AFTER READING

From your reading of *Mizilca* and *Philbert The Fearful* decide which of the following sentences describes the behaviour of Mizilca and Philbert in the stories, and write them on to your chart under the heading BEHAVIOUR.

— begs to leave home

— is very cautious

— can ride, fight and shoot a bow and arrow

— shows no fear

— would rather use tricks than fists to fight

— enjoys a quiet and comfortable life

Both Mizilca and Philbert are successful in what they set out to do. Which of the following qualities do (a) both characters; (b) either character show in achieving their aims?

When you have decided, write them on to your chart under the heading QUALITIES.

good looks	kindness
intelligence	bravery
quick wittedness	persistence
imagination	humour
strength	honesty

For Writing

In the stories you have read in this book so far the writers have changed one or more of the usual conventions. For example they have changed

— the typical elements;
— the events (plot)
— the characters;
— the style of writing

Choose a fairy story or folk tale you know yourself and write your own changed version of it. You might find it helpful to make a plan like the one below:

TRADITIONAL STORY SNOW WHITE	MY CHANGED VERSION EBONY BLACK
Beginning: Once upon a time in a faraway kingdom. . . **Main Events:** 1. There is a princess called Snow White 2. She has a jealous stepmother who has a magic mirror	**Beginning:** It 'appen one time inna country far away **Main Events:** 1. There is a princess called Ebony Black 2. She has a jealous mother who has a computer

2. SEE HOW THEY CHANGE...

Re-writing Isn't New

Making changes to fairy stories and folk tales is nothing new. Stories were first told to people out loud. They were not written down, but were passed mostly by word of mouth by travellers and story-tellers, who changed the stories to suit people listening.

Although the stories they told were meant to be entertaining, they also had other purposes. For example, one of the most common kind of story was the story that gives a warning. Stories which warn children about dangers are to be found all over the world. Children in these stories are threatened by wild animals, by giants, ogres and witches or evil spirits. Even though the stories were about fantastic things that could never really happen, there were 'messages' in them about sensible ways of behaving. For example: it is dangerous to walk alone in a dark place. Or: it is dangerous to let a stranger into your house.

Probably the most common dangers children face in fairy and folk stories are listed on the chart below.

Make a list of stories that you know in which these different dangers are to be found.

CHILDREN IN DANGER FROM. . .	STORIES I REMEMBER. . .
Giants and ogres	
Witches	
Evil spirits	
Wild animals	

When fairy stories and folk tales came to be written down the writers didn't just write them straight down as they heard them. They also made changes to suit their own ideas and to suit the readers they had in mind.

So writers might:

- shorten the story

- use different words to make the story sound 'posher'

- leave out rude bits

- leave out bloodthirsty bits

- change the names, jobs and ages of the characters

- change the place in which the story is set

- change the way characters behave

- change the story so that their readers would get a particular 'message' from it.

Red Riding Hood

It is interesting to look at different versions of the same story which have been written by different people at different times.

In this section there are five different versions of the story of *Red Riding Hood*. Read them all and notice any differences you can see between them.

Try to think: what kind of readers did the writer have in mind?

Comparing the Versions

The chart below is to help you make notes on the character of Red Riding Hood in each of the five versions, and on the end of each story.

To help you get started, some words you could use to describe Red Riding Hood and the story endings are listed below.

CHARACTER/BEHAVIOUR
OF RED RIDING HOOD

weak
strong
brave
frightened
smart
sweet
simple
independent
thoughtful
obedient

ENDINGS

happy
sad
violent
funny
hopeful
moralistic
serious

	CHARACTER/BEHAVIOUR OF RED RIDING HOOD	ENDINGS
Story 1		
Story 2		Violent. Moralistic. Sad
Story 3	Sweet Simple	
Story 4		
Story 5		

32

Red Riding Hood
1

There was a woman who had made some bread. She said to her daughter, "Go carry this hot loaf and a bottle of milk to your granny."

So the little girl departed. At the crossway she met *bzou*, the werewolf, who said to her,

"Where are you going?"

"I'm taking this hot loaf and a bottle of milk to my granny."

"What path are you taking?", said the werewolf, "the path of needles or the path of pins?".

"The path of needles," the little girl said.

"All right, then I'll take the path of pins".

The little girl entertained herself by gathering needles. Meanwhile the werewolf arrived at the grandmother's house, killed her, put some of her meat in the cupboard and a bottle of blood on the shelf. The little girl arrived and knocked at the door.

"Push the door," said the werewolf, "it's barred by a piece of wet straw."

"Good day, granny, I've brought you a hot loaf and a bottle of milk."

"Put it in the cupboard, my child. Take some of the meat which is inside and the bottle of wine on the shelf."

"Undress yourself, my child," the werewolf said, "and come lie down beside me."

"Where should I put my apron?".

"Throw it into the fire, my child, you won't be needing it anymore."

When she laid herself down in the bed, the little girl said,

"Oh, Granny, how hairy you are!"

"The better to keep myself warm, my child!"

"Oh, Granny, what big nails you have!"

"The better to scratch myself with, my child!"

"Oh, Granny, what big shoulders you have!"

"The better to carry the firewood, my child!"

"Oh, Granny, what big ears you have!"

"The better to hear you with, my child!"

"Oh, Granny, what big nostrils you have!"

"The better to snuff my tobacco with, my child!"

"Oh, Granny, what a big mouth you have!"

"The better to eat you with, my child!"

"Oh, Granny, I've got to go badly. Let me go outside."

"Do it in the bed, my child!"

"Oh, no, I want to go outside."

"All right, but make it quick."

The werewolf attached a woollen rope to her foot and let her go outside.

When the little girl was outside, she tied the end of the rope to a plum tree in the courtyard. The werewolf became impatient and said, "Are you making a load out there? Are you making a load?"

When he realized that nobody was answering him, he jumped out of bed and saw that the little girl had escaped. He followed her but arrived at her house just at the moment she entered.

Red Riding Hood
2

Once upon a time there was a little village girl, the prettiest that had ever been seen. Her mother doted on her, and her grandmother even more. This good woman made her a little red hood which suited her so well that she was called Little Red Riding Hood wherever she went.

One day, after her mother had baked some biscuits, she said to Little Red Riding Hood, "Go see how your grandmother is feeling, for I have heard that she is sick. Take her some biscuits and this small pot of butter." Little Red Riding Hood departed at once to visit her grandmother, who lived in another village. In passing through a wood she met old neighbour wolf, who had a great desire to eat her. But he did not dare because of some woodcutters who were in the forest. He asked her where she was going. The poor child, who did not know that it is dangerous to stop and listen to a wolf, said to him, "I am going to see my grandmother, and I am bringing some biscuits with a small pot of butter which my mother has sent her."

"Does she live far from here?" asked the wolf.

"Oh, yes!" said Little Red Riding Hood. "You must pass the mill which you can see right over there, and hers is the first house in the village."

"Well, then," said the wolf. "I want to go and see her, too. I'll take this path here, and you take that path there, and we'll see who'll get there first."

The wolf began to run as fast as he could on the path which was shorter, and the little girl took the longer path, and she enjoyed herself by gathering nuts, running after butterflies, and making bouquets of small flowers which she found. It did not take the wolf long to arrive at the grandmother's house, He knocked: Toc, toc.

"Who's there?"

"It's your granddaughter, Little Red Riding Hood," said the wolf, disguising his voice, "I've brought you some biscuits and a little pot of butter which my mother has sent you."

The good grandmother, who was in her bed because she was not feeling well, cried out to him, "Pull the bobbin, and the latch will fall."

The wolf pulled the bobbin, and the door opened. He threw himself upon the good woman and devoured her quicker than a wink, for it had been more than three days since he had last eaten. After that he closed the door and lay down in the grandmother's bed to wait for Little Red Riding Hood, who after a while came knocking at the door. Toc, toc.

"Who's there?"

When she heard the gruff voice of the wolf, Little Red Riding Hood was scared at first, but, believing that her grandmother had a cold, she responded, "It's your granddaughter, Little Red Riding Hood. I've brought you some biscuits and a little pot of butter which my mother has sent you."

The wolf softened his voice and cried out to her, "Pull the bobbin, and the latch will fall."

Little Red Riding Hood pulled the bobbin, and the door opened.

Upon seeing her enter, the wolf hid himself under the bedcovers and said to her, "Put the biscuits and the pot of butter on the bin and come lie down beside me."

Little Red Riding Hood undressed and went to get into bed, where she was quite astonished to see the way her grandmother was dressed in her nightgown. She said to her: "What big arms you have, grandmother!"

"The better to hug you with, my child."

"What big legs you have, grandmother!"

"The better to run with, my child."

"What big ears you have, grandmother!"

"The better to hear you with, my child."

"What big eyes you have, grandmother!"

"The better to see you with, my child."

"What big teeth you have, grandmother!"

"The better to eat you."

And upon saying these words, the wicked wolf threw himself upon Little Red Riding Hood and ate her up.

Red Riding Hood
3

Once upon a time there was a sweet little maiden. Whoever laid eyes upon her could not help but love her. But it was her grandmother who loved her most. She could never give the child enough. One time she made a present, a small, red velvet cap, and, since it was so becoming, she always wanted to wear only this. So she was simply called Little Red Cap.

One day her mother said to her, "Come, Little Red Cap, take this piece of cake and a bottle of wine and bring them to your grandmother. She is sick and weak. This will strengthen her. Be nice and good, and give her my regards. Don't tarry on your way, and don't stray from the path, otherwise you'll fall and break the glass. Then your sick grandmother will get nothing."

Little Red Cap promised her mother to be very obedient. Well, the grandmother lived out in the woods, half an hour from the village. And, as soon as Little Red Cap entered the woods, she encountered the wolf. However, Little Red Cap did not know what a wicked sort of an animal he was and was not afraid of him.

"Good day, Little Red Cap."

"Thank you kindly, wolf."

"Where are you going so early, Little Red Cap?"

"To Grandmother's."

"What are you carrying under your apron?"

"My grandmother is sick and weak, so I'm bringing her cake and wine. We baked yesterday, and this will strengthen her."

"Where does your grandmother live, Little Red Cap?"

"Another quarter of an hour from here in the woods. Her house is under the three big oak trees. You can tell it by the hazel bushes," said Little Red Cap.

The wolf thought to himself, this is a good juicy morsel for me. How are you going to manage to get her?"

"Listen, Little Red Cap," he said, "have you seen the pretty flowers which are in the woods? Why don't you look around you? I believe that you haven't even noticed how lovely the birds are singing. You march along as if you were going straight to school in the village, and it is so delightful out here in the woods."

Little Red Cap looked around and saw how the sun had broken through the trees and everything around her was filled with beautiful flowers. So she thought to herself: Well, if I were to bring grandmother a bunch of flowers, she would like that. It's still early, and I'll arrive on time. So she plunged into the woods and looked for flowers. And each time she plucked one, she believed she saw another one even prettier and ran after it further and further into the woods. But the wolf went straight to the grandmother's house and knocked at the door.

"Who's there outside?"

"Little Red Cap. I'm bringing you cake and wine. Open up."

"Just lift the latch," the grandmother called. "I'm too weak and can't get up."

The wolf lifted the latch, and the door sprung open. Then he went straight inside to the grandmother's bed and swallowed her. Next he took her clothes, put them on with her nightcap, lay down in her bed, and drew the curtains.

Little Red Cap had been running around after flowers, and, only when she had as many as she could carry, did she continue on her way to her grandmother. Upon arriving there she found the door open. This puzzled her, and, as she entered the room, it seemed so strange inside that she thought, Oh, oh, my God, how frightened I feel today, and usually I like to be at grandmother's. Whereupon she went to the bed and drew back the curtains. Her grandmother lay there with her cap pulled down over her face so that it gave her a strange appearance.

"Oh, grandmother, what big ears you have!"

"The better to hear you with."

"Oh, grandmother, what big eyes you have!"

"The better to see you with."

"Oh, grandmother, what big hands you have!"

"The better to grab you with."

"Oh, grandmother, what a terrible big mouth you have!"

"The better to eat you with."

With that the wolf jumped out of bed, leapt on Little Red Cap and swallowed her. After the wolf had digested the juicy morsel, he lay down in bed again, fell asleep, and began to snore very loudly. The hunter happened to be passing by and wondered to himself about the old lady's snoring, You had better take a look. Then he went inside, and, when he came to the bed, he found the wolf whom he had been hunting for a long time. He had certainly eaten the grandmother. Perhaps she can still be saved. I won't shoot, thought the hunter. Then he took a shearing knife and slit the wolf's belly open, and, after he had made a couple of cuts, he saw the glowing red cap, and, after he made a few more cuts, the girl jumped out and cried, "Oh, how frightened I was! It was so dark in the wolf's body." And then the grandmother came out alive. So now Little Red Cap fetched large heavy stones with which they filled the wolf's body, and, when he awoke, he wanted to jump up, but the stones were so heavy that he fell down dead.

So all three were pleased. The hunter skinned the fur from the wolf. The grandmother ate the cake and drank the wine that Little Red Cap had brought, and Little Red Cap thought to herself: Never again in your life will you stray by yourself in the woods when your mother has forbidden it.

Red Riding Hood
4

One afternoon a big wolf waited in a dark forest for a little girl to come along carrying a basket of food to her grandmother. Finally a little girl did come along and she was carrying a basket of food. "Are you carrying that basket to your grandmother?" asked the wolf. The little girl says yes, she was. So the wolf asked her where her grandmother lived and the little girl told him and he disappeared into the wood.

When the little girl opened the door of her grandmother's house she saw that there was somebody in bed with a nightcap on. She had approached no nearer than twenty-five feet from the bed when she saw that it was not her grandmother but the wolf, for even in a nightcap a wolf does not look any more like your grandmother than the Metro-Goldwyn lion looks like Calvin Coolidge. So the little girl took an automatic out of her basket and shot the wolf dead.

Moral: It is not so easy to fool little girls nowadays as it used to be.

Red Riding Hood
5

In the far north, beside a river which froze hard as rock in the dark days of winter, there stood a great timber mill and a town built out of wood. The wood came from the trees of the deep forest which surrounded the town and stretched into the far distance.

In this town lived a quiet and shy little girl, called Red Riding Hood. Her real name was Nadia but everyone called her Red Riding Hood because when the cold came she always wore a thick red cloak with a hood. It had been given to her by her great-grandmother who had worn it herself, long ago, when she was a child.

Her great-grandmother still lived in a cottage in the forest and Red Riding Hood loved to visit her more than anything in the world; but she would never go alone because she was frightened to walk through the forest.

Red Riding Hood was frightened of many things. She was frightened of going up to bed by herself, she was frightened of dogs and of thunder and of people she did not know. But she was most frightened of the forest. The forest seemed strange to her for she had been born far away in a city in the south, where her mother and father had gone to be trained for their work in the great timber mill.

"Why do you never play in the forest like we did when we were children?" they asked her.

"It is dark under the trees," said Red Riding Hood, "and in

winter the wolves howl in the distance."

"There have been no wolves in the forest since anyone can remember," said her parents, laughing.

But her great-grandmother took the child to one side and said to her quietly, "Not everyone can hear that howling; they think it is only the wind in the trees. One winter day when I was a girl, out alone chopping wood for the stove, I was attacked by one of the grey wolves which speak."

"Oh, great-grandmother!" whispered Red Riding Hood. "What did you do?"

"I fought the wolf with my hatchet and killed it." replied the old woman, "for I was strong and agile when I was young."

But now the great-grandmother was very old and frail, and almost every day when school and work were over, Red Riding Hood went with her mother and father, or with some of the other children, to cook supper for her and to sit and talk.

Winter was coming. Snow fell. It was dark before the children came out of school and the wind grew icy cold.

In the school the children were hard at work finishing the fur jackets which they had been making to wear during the bitter weather. They were very proud of these jackets, for all of them had cut out their own with great sharp knives and were sewing pieces together with special strong needles and thread. Only Red Riding Hood was not making a jacket. She wanted to wear her red cloak and hood and besides she was frightened that she might cut herself on one of the sharp knives.

Her mother and father worried that she would be cold without a jacket, for the red cloak was growing worn.

"We can see to that," said the great-grandmother, as they all sat around her stove one evening. "Bring the special sewing things with you after school tomorrow and I will help you make a sheepskin lining for your cloak."

"What a good idea," said Red Riding Hood's parents and Red Riding Hood thought happily about tomorrow as she walked home between them through the forest.

"Why don't you take some presents to great-grandmother?" said the father the next morning. "Here are some brown eggs and some chocolate and a pot of the blackberry jam you helped us make." "We shall be busy this evening," said her mother, "but you can easily walk to great-grandmother's on your own. The path through the forest is cleared of snow every day and there will be a full moon tonight."

Red Riding Hood said nothing. She took a basket and carefully put into it the eggs, the chocolate and the jam. She did not feel happy any more. The other children were going to stay late at school to finish their jackets. She would have to walk through the forest to her great-grandmother's cottage all alone.

Red Riding Hood was frightened. All day at school she could think about nothing but whether she dared to walk through the forest alone. At dinnertime she did not want to eat because she felt sick. She borrowed a special needle and thread and a sharp knife and put them in the basket with the presents, but when school was over she did not set out for her great-grandmother's, although she was longing to see her. She turned her back on the forest and started to walk into the town towards home.

It was dark and quiet outside the school. The other children were still inside sewing their jackets. In the distance Red Riding Hood could hear the noise of sawing from the timber mill. Then she heard another sound, from quite close, somewhere near the edge of the forest. It was the howling of a wolf.

Red Riding Hood stood listening. She knew it was one of the grey wolves. But who would believe her? They would laugh and say she had imagined it. She thought of her great-grandmother, all alone.

What if a wolf had come again for her now that she was no longer young and agile? Red Riding Hood turned around and ran into the forest and along the path to the old woman's cottage.

She ran and ran until her side hurt and her heart thumped so fast she had to stop to get some breath.

The moon shone through the bare branches of the trees onto the snow and the frozen earth. It was very still. Then a gust of wind blew snow into the air and through the wind Red Riding Hood thought she heard a cold voice calling, "Run home, little girl, run home. This is the night of the wolf."

Then she heard a low growl, and staring through the flurry of snow she saw a streak of grey moving toward great-grandmother's cottage.

Her mouth went dry and her legs felt as if she could not move them, but she made them walk on until at last she reached the cottage.

"Great-grandmother, great-grandmother!" she cried, rattling the door latch. "I'm here!"

"Lift up the latch and walk in," called a thin and quavering voice.

"Great-grandmother, are you ill?" cried little Red Riding Hood, and she opened the door and ran into the bedroom.

In the high, wooden bed there was a shape huddled down under the bedclothes. It was hard to see with only the moonlight coming through the window. Red Riding Hood peered at the shape and moved closer to the bed.

"What big eyes you have, great-grandmother," she said.

"All the better to see with, my dear," said the thin, quavering voice.

"And what big ears you have, great-grandmother."

"All the better to hear you with, my dear," said the voice.

"And what a strange nose you have, great-grandmother," said Red Riding Hood, moving a little closer.

"All the better to smell you with, my dear," said the voice, and Red Riding Hood could see a mouth full of yellow pointed teeth.

"And what big teeth you have!" she cried, backing away.

"All the better to eat you with!" snarled the shape, leaping from the bed. It was a grey wolf.

Red Riding Hood screamed and as she screamed she heard her great-grandmother calling. "Quick, child, quick! Let me in!"

Red Riding Hood flung open the door into the kitchen and there was her great-grandmother pulling a blazing branch from the stove. With this branch she advanced on the growling wolf, old and bent though she was.

The wolf was frightened by the flame. It circled fiercely around the old woman, trying to get behind her and spring on her. Red Riding Hood shrank back against the wall. She could see that soon the branch would be burnt out and then the wolf would spring on her great-grandmother. Suddenly she remembered how easily the other children had cut through skins to make their jackets. She reached into her basket and pulled out the great sharp knife. Just as the branch burnt out and the wolf gathered itself for the kill, Red Riding Hood leapt forward and plunged the knife deep into its heart. The wolf gave one terrifying snarl and fell dead on the ground in a pool of blood.

With the help of her great-grandmother Red Riding Hood skinned the wolf and together they made a lining of its fur. "Listen, great-granddaughter," said the old woman, as they worked together stitching the lining into the red cloak, "this cloak now has special powers. Whenever you meet another child who is shy and timid, lend that child the cloak to wear as you play together in the forest, and then, like you, they will grow brave."

So whenever she met such a child, Red Riding Hood did as her great-grandmother had said, but the rest of the time she wore the cloak herself and for many years it kept her warm as she explored deeper and deeper into the great forest.

Red Riding Hood

In the stories you have just read you will have noticed that the girl is called by different names. But in the descriptions of the different versions that follow she is always referred to as Red Riding Hood and the animal is always referred to as the wolf.

Read through the descriptions and see if you can match them to the versions of *Red Riding Hood* that you have just read.

You should be able to explain your decisions by giving examples from the different versions.

a. This *Red Riding Hood* was written by Perrault in 1697. It was written for upper class readers in France and it shows how adults of that class thought about children as quite different from themselves. This was unlike the view held by parents of the peasant class at that time, where children were seen as young adults whose work was very important to help the family survive.

The little girl in Perrault's version doesn't seem capable of being much help to anyone — not even herself. She is punished not because of her helplessness however, but because she behaves very badly by talking to a stranger.

The language of the story is more formal and the improper or rude bits have been left out, because polite, young upper class girls should not read or hear about such vulgar things.

b. This version was written by women in Liverpool in 1972. They wanted to show that Little Red Riding Hood could be brave and capable, but they also show that this is not always easy. The wolf is presented as very frightening and a very real danger to Red Riding Hood and her grandmother.

In the end the two women defeat the wolf together but first, Red Riding Hood has to overcome her own fears and to learn that she can be independent and rely on her own strength and abilities.

c. This version of *Red Riding Hood* is probably closest to the way the story would have been told before it was written down. It would have been told by storytellers to ordinary people, young and old — villagers, farm workers and peasants — for entertainment. So although a warning is given in it to children to beware of strangers, the main aim is not to teach them right from wrong or how 'nice' children should behave. In fact there are some quite gruesome details in the story and at times the language is not very polite.

Red Riding Hood herself is independent, cheerful and self-reliant, which is probably how the children listening to the story were expected to be. From an early age they would have been working quite hard to help support their families.

d. This version was written in the nineteenth century by the Brothers Grimm. The story is made sweeter and nicer for children to read. The moral lesson is clear, but so that children reading it won't be upset by a violent ending, the heroine is given another chance to think about how nice young girls should behave.

Although the story still has the purpose of warning children about strangers, it also provides a model of good behaviour and manners for young ladies. Red Riding Hood in this version is pretty, sweet, lovable, obedient, nervous and far from quick-witted.

e. This version was written in 1939 by James Thurber. In it he sets out to make fun of the earlier very 'proper' stories of *Red Riding Hood*. He does this by making the reader laugh at the most unlikely part of the story: the wolf disguising himself as the grandmother and completely fooling Red Riding Hood. In Thurber's story she is not tricked for a minute, and takes very direct action against the wolf.

Red Riding Hood

FOR WRITING

The five versions of *Red Riding Hood* that you have just read are in order from the earliest to the most modern.

Which version did you like best and why?

Look at the notes you made on each of the stories and write about the way *Red Riding Hood* has changed over the years, and why you think the changes have occurred.

The Collectors

Writers did change stories to suit the ideas around at their time, but this is not the only reason that the early written-down versions of fairy stories and folk tales so often seem to be about girls who are weak and silly, and about boys who are brave and adventurous.

This is what one writer has to say:

In the fairy tales we know best today, the heroes seem to have all the interesting adventures. They get to kill dragons and outwit giants and rescue princesses and find the magic treasure. As for the heroines, things just happen to them: they are persecuted by wicked stepmothers, eaten by wolves, or fall asleep for a hundred years. All most of them ever seem to do is wait patiently for the right prince to come, or for someone else to rescue them from dangers and enchantments. This has made some people say that modern children ought not to read fairy tales, because they will get the idea that girls are supposed to be beautiful and good and helpless and dull.

But there are thousands of folktales in the world that are not at all like this. They have heroines who can fight and hunt as well as any man, heroines who defeat giants, answer riddles, outwit the Devil, and rescue their friends and relatives from all sorts of dangers and evil spells. They are not only beautiful and good, but also strong, brave, clever, and resourceful.

Why don't we know these stories as well as the others? It is because the first collections of fairy tales for children were put together over a hundred years ago, when women and girls were supposed to be weak and helpless; and the editors who picked the stories out of the many that were available chose ones like *Snow White*, *Cinderella*, *Sleeping Beauty*, and *Little Red Riding-Hood*. These tales were printed over and over again, while the rest were almost forgotten.

Most of the editors who chose these stories were men. The original tellers of folktales, on the other hand, were mainly women. And they were not frail Victorian ladies, but working women: farmers' wives, shopkeepers, craftswomen, household servants, children's nurses, and midwives. They lived active, interesting lives, and the stories they told show it.

Alison Lurie

3. DOING GOOD OR ELSE...

Two Sisters and Two Bowls
How Crab Got Its Back
Prince of Nettles

Two Sisters and Two Bowls

Long ago there lived a rich man of the Ibo tribe. He owned a big herd of cattle, and he had two wives. The daughter of his chief wife was a pretty girl, but she was proud and lazy, but N'Gozi, the daughter of his other wife, was gentle, kind and a good worker as well.

"Go now, O my daughters, and collect wood for the fire," said the head wife one day to the two girls. They went. They began to gather firewood, but, as they gathered, they wandered far. At last they noticed that they were a long way from home, and that quite soon it would be night. Then they saw that, farther on among the trees, there was a hut. Not a village — just one hut. Outside this hut was an old woman. The girls were beginning to be afraid, for they heard how the leopards and lions were beginning to roar and to cough and to rumble, Huh! Huh! coughed the leopards.

"Where do you come from, O my daughters?" asked the old woman. They told her.

"That's far away," said she, and shook her head. "Soon it will be dark and the beasts of the forest will come out to hunt."

"That, O mother, is just what we are afraid of," said the girls. "We hear them already."

"You must come into my hut, O my daughters, and you must stay till light comes again and the beasts go back to their lairs," said the old woman.

48

So they thanked her and she led them into her hut and made the door fast.

Then the old woman got ready two dinners. One was a platter of fine food! High food! Very best! But on the other dish was poor, low food, miserable to see! The old woman held out both of them, and the proud girl reached out her hand and took the platter of high food. Her sister, N'Gozi, looked at the other one, then she too reached out her hand. As she ate she whispered to her sister, "I didn't refuse this food! I could not disappoint the old woman! She is kind!"

When the two girls had eaten, the old woman made up two beds. One was soft and high; the other was wider, but it was very hard! Very low! It was just a thin mat on the ground. Quickly, and without a word, the proud girl jumped up into the soft, good bed. So the old woman and the other girl lay down on the hard, low bed on the floor.

In the morning the proud girl slept on, in her soft, high bed, but her sister and the old woman got up early and the old woman rolled up their bed and began to sweep the hut.

"Mother, let me help you!" said N'Gozi, and while the old woman began to get them some breakfast, this girl, N'Gozi, swept and tidied everything nicely. But the proud girl did not stir in her bed! No! She did not open her eyes till the food was brought. Once more it was the good food, the high food, that she chose, while her sister and the old woman ate the poor food! Low food! When they had eaten it, it was N'Gozi who washed the platters, and, once more, made everything neat in the hut.

So at last, when they were ready to go, the old woman brought out two bowls. Made out of gourds were these bowls, and covers were tied tightly over them so that the girls could not see what was inside.

"These are my presents to you, my daughters," said the old woman. "But you must each promise not to open your present till you get to the village again and to your home." Both girls thanked her and both promised.

On the way back the proud girl wanted to open hers. She was sure that it must be something nice that the old woman had given her. But her sister, N'Gozi, persuaded her.

"We both promised," said she.

At last they were in their own village again, near their father's compound. Then the proud girl wouldn't wait any more. She began to tear the covering off her bowl.

Oh, what a sight! It was terrible. Something poured out of the bowl that was like a yellow smoke. It was something that clung to the girl — something that made the proud girl's face so ugly it was dreadful to look at!

But when her sister, N'Gozi, opened hers, everything nice that you can think of flowed out of that bowl. It was like water flowing out in a stream, only this was a stream of presents. Bead necklaces! Red and green! Bracelets and anklets made of polished shell and of gold with little bells that tinkled! Finely woven mats and baskets and, last of all, came a tiny hut that grew big, and then big again, as soon as it touched the ground.

Well, the story of the magic bowl soon got round, and when she came out from her new hut, her very own hut, N'Gozi looked so pretty, wearing all those necklaces, anklets and bracelets, that a dozen of the handsomest of the young men in the village wanted to marry her.

"This girl," they said, "whose mother had taught her such nice manners! This girl who is pretty and so lucky! This girl who owns such a nice hut!"

So N'Gozi chose the young man she liked best.

As for her proud sister, no one except her own mother, the head wife, could bear to look at her, and she didn't ever get a husband. This, O my people, is my tale.

How Crab Got Its Back

In a village there once lived two sisters who were as different from each other as chalk from cheese.

Esmeralda, the younger sister, was plain as plain could be, but she was kind to everyone and worked from morning till night scrubbing and cleaning their little house so that it was as neat as a pin. Yolanda, the elder sister, was the most beautiful girl in the village, but she was proud and haughty and never a finger would she lift to help her sister.

One day Esmeralda went to the river to fill her goblet and she saw, sitting at the water's edge, a strange old woman. Around the woman's waist was wrapped a towel, but her back was bare and she was trying to scoop up water in her thin, wasted hands to wash her back.

When she saw Esmeralda she began to sing in a voice that was high and shrill:

"Scratch my back, daughter, oh!
Wash it well with water, oh!"

Esmeralda saw that the old woman's back was lined and very sore and she felt very sorry for her, although the old woman's back felt as hard as board, Esmeralda scratched it and washed it until her nails were broken. But as soon as she stopped the old woman began to complain and to sing:

"Scratch my back, daughter, oh!
Wash it well with water, oh!"

And although the old woman's back felt as sharp as broken bottles, Ermeralda scratched it and washed it until her hands were bleeding.

Then the old woman said in a voice as gentle as a pigeon's cooing, "Child, you have been patient and kind to a miserable old woman and I should like to give you something in return. What do you wish for most?"

Esmeralda felt ashamed to ask anything of one who seemed so much in need, so she replied, "Just your blessing, mother."

"Well," said the old woman, "you may have that and more. Look in the water, Esmeralda, and you shall see what you will be!"

Imagine Esmeralda's surprise when she looked in the water and saw not her plain face but the most beautiful, the kindest face she had ever seen. She raised her head to thank the old woman but the old woman had vanished.

At first Yolanda could not believe that this beautiful girl was indeed Esmeralda whom she had scorned and ill-treated all her life. She was green with envy, and without waiting to hear the whole story she rushed down to the river, for she thought, "Stupid Ermeralda! Where does she think a pretty face will get her? I shall ask for great wealth. Then I shan't have to share that pigs' pen with her!"

As Yolanda went down to the river she saw, sitting at the water's edge, the ugliest old woman she had ever set eyes on. Her hands and feet were shrivelled until they looked like claws, and her bare back was crossed by so many lines that it looked as though it were cracked all over. When the old woman saw Yolanda she began to sing in a voice that was high and shrill:

"Scratch my back, daughter, oh!
Wash it well with water, oh!"

But Yolanda was in a fever of impatience to find the source of her sister's good fortune. Nor did she know that she had found it, for she had only one wicked thought in her head.

"Out of my way, you ugly creature!" she cried. "Do you expect me to wallow in the mud with you! Scratch your back with those claws of yours!" And she pushed the old woman to one side.

"Insolent girl!" said the old woman. "As you see *me* so shall *you* be!"

And at that moment Yolanda became an ugly creature, her limbs shrivelled up and turned into her claws and her back became hard and cracked all over.

She cannot now bear to be seen, for she remembers that once she was beautiful. So she wallows in the mud and hides away under rocks and cliffs. And when sand and mud fill the cracks and her back itches, she rushes down to the river to wash it off for no one will scratch her back.

Two Sisters and Two Bowls, How Crab Got Its Back

Discuss the following statements about the stories. Then decide if the statements about the stories are **exactly the same, nearly the same** or **different** for each story, and put a tick in the right column.

	EXACTLY THE SAME	NEARLY THE SAME	DIFFERENT
1. There is a good natured, helpful and obedient girl.			
2. There is a lazy, proud and bad tempered girl.			
3. The good natured, helpful and obedient girl helps an old woman.			
4. The lazy, proud and bad tempered girl refuses to help an old woman.			
5. The good natured, helpful and obedient girl is rewarded.			
6. The lazy, proud and bad tempered girl is punished.			
7. The rewards involve beauty, great wealth and a handsome husband.			
8. The punishments involve pain, being made ugly and finally death.			

If these stories are meant to teach children, especially girls, how to "behave properly", which of the following "lessons" do you think they would be expected to learn?

1. You should always behave in a kind way to others.

2. You should be kind to people only until you have got what you want from them.

3. It doesn't matter how you behave towards other people as long as you get what you want.

4. If you behave badly to others you will be punished.

5. If you are kind to others you will be rewarded.

6. You should always be nice and obedient.

Prince of Nettles

BEFORE READING

You are going to read a story which contains the following elements:

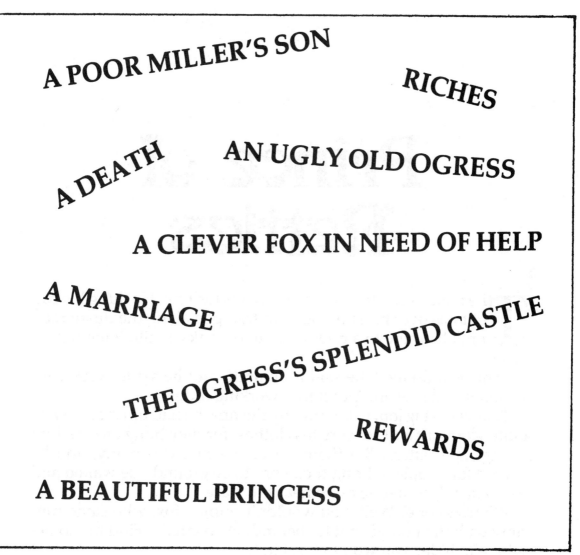

A POOR MILLER'S SON

RICHES

A DEATH

AN UGLY OLD OGRESS

A CLEVER FOX IN NEED OF HELP

A MARRIAGE

THE OGRESS'S SPLENDID CASTLE

REWARDS

A BEAUTIFUL PRINCESS

In your pair or group make up a story that includes these characters and events. Or discuss how you think a story with these characters and events in it might go.

Prince of Nettles

The miller's son left home to seek his fortune. He flung his bag of tools over his shoulder and tramped along the dusty road until he came to a river and on its banks a mill, lying half in ruins.

"This will do me," he said to himself, and he set to work with hammer and saw and put it into working order.

That was a big job, to be sure. By the time he had finished he was quite worn out and so were his clothes, for they hung around him in rags and tatters. But there it was: his mill was ready, and he waited for people to bring their corn to be ground. He waited and he waited, but no-one came near the place.

What, no-one? Well, you wouldn't count a fox, who came running with the hounds not far behind. He panted, "Find me somewhere to hide. You won't regret it."

"Get under that sack," said the miller, and when the hunt turned up a few minutes later he sent them off the wrong way.

"Thank you, miller," said the fox when danger was passed. "I'll do you a good turn too. How would you like a nice little wife?"

"A fine chance I have of that," said the miller. "Just look at me! No money, and only the rags I stand up in, No girl, nice or otherwise, would give me a second look."

"We'll see about that," said the fox, and he trotted off. He was back before long with a bit of copper in his jaws. "Hold on to this," he said. "It will come in useful before long."

Next day the fox came again, this time with a large chunk of gold. "Put this in a safe place," he said, and was away in a flash of his bushy tail. Two days later he returned, and now he brought a fine diamond. "Now it won't be long," he said. "It is high time we did something about this wife for you. You can leave everything in my capable paws. Just give me the bit of copper."

Away went the fox at a brisk trot and he did not stop until he came to the king's court. "Greetings, Your Majesty," he said. "I hear that you have a daughter and no husband for her yet. My master, Prince Csihan, sends this small gift of copper. He is looking for a wife, and your girl might perhaps suit him."

"Bring him along and let me have a look at him," said the king. "Here, take him this ring as my goodwill gift."

Back trotted the fox to the mill. "Cheer up, miller," he said. "You have a new name now. You are Prince Csihan. Don't forget it. A very good name it is too, seeing that the mill garden is nothing but nettles. The king sends you this ring and invites you to visit his court to pay your repects to the princess. If you do exactly what I say, you are made. Now give me that gold. I'll take it to the king so that he will know that you are a man of substance."

The fox was back at the palace early next day. "Good news, Your Majesty," he said. "My prince is disposed to like this match, and he sends you this gold to help with the wedding expenses. He is sorry that he has no smaller change, but all his gold comes in lumps as big as this."

"Well, well," said the king. "This seems to be a fine prince. He will do nicely for my daughter."

Now the fox returned to the miller. "Tomorrow we shall make your fortune, my fine Prince of Nettles," he said. "Be ready early." And indeed next morning they set out at dawn. After a long walk they came in sight of a great castle. "There," said the fox. "How does that suit you? There lives your bride."

Then he gave the miller a long hard look. "You had better take off those clothes," he said. "They are fit for nothing but burning." And when the rags were gone, "Into the river with you, and have a good bath." So that is what the miller did.

"Now wait here and don't move until I send for you," and the fox left the miller in the forest and trotted off to the king.

"Oh unlucky day!" he panted. "We set off in state in a carriage drawn by six fine horses and with three waggons laden with gifts for Your Majesty, but robbers set on us as we came through the forest, and everything is gone. The prince himself has been stripped to his skin, and I have had to leave him hiding his shame in the woods. All he had left in the world is this diamond, and he has sent it to you for a wedding gift to his bride."

At once the king called for a carriage and horses, and he found robes fit for a prince. Then they drove off to the forest, and the fox took the robes and found the miller cowering in the bushes. "Here, put these on quickly," he said, "and for goodness sake wear them as if you are used to such finery. The king is waiting."

When they reached the court the king took the miller by the hand. "My dear son," he said. "How I grieve for your misfortune! But do not despair. Your troubles are at an end. The priest is waiting, and he will marry you to my daughter with no more delay."

So the wedding took place, and the feasting went on for many days. The miller went about in a daze but he liked his new wife very well, and the comfort and good living were equally to his liking. He felt that he had nothing more to wish for.

But one day the princess said to him: "Dearest, isn't it time that we went to see your kingdom? Your subjects must be longing to see their prince again."

Well, that took the polish off the prince's pleasure! He went off very reluctantly to the stables to prepare for the journey. There was the fox, stretched out at his ease in the straw, and the miller's tears began to fall in earnest when he saw him.

"What's your trouble, my nettly prince?" said the fox.

"It's the princess," said the miller. "She wants to visit my kingdom. What am I to do?"

"Don't you worry. Just get ready for the journey."

So they prepared a carriage, and loaded three waggons with all the treasure that had been given at the wedding. Then they set out.

The fox scampered on ahead. Soon he came upon herdsmen driving a great herd of oxen. "Whose beasts are these?" he said. "They belong to our mistress, the ogress," they said. "If anyone asks you," said the fox, "tell them that they belong to Prince Csihan."

Then he ran on to the ogress's castle. "Let me in quickly, mother," he gasped.

"Lucky for you that you called me mother!" growled the huge old woman. "Otherwise I'd have ground your bones to poppy-seed."

"Never mind about that," said the fox. "I came to warn you that an army is on its way to capture you."

"I must hide," said the ogress.

"Come with me. I know just the place," and the fox took her to a cave on the shores of a deep lake. "There, wash your face here and I will return when danger is past."

The fox ran back to the miller. "Come on," he said. "Your palace is waiting." And he led the way to the ogress's castle, where everything, although rather on the big side, was as rich and plentiful as even a princess could wish.

When the happy couple were safely asleep that night, the fox went back to the ogress. "I heard the noise of horses," she said. "The army can't be far away. Isn't there somewhere safer that I can hide?"

"Come this way," said the fox. He led her through the darkness to a cliff-top above the lake. Then he went behind her and gave her a sharp push. Into the lake she went and was drowned. The fox returned to the castle, and now there was no-one to question the right of Prince Csihan and his bride to live there.

The miller was well pleased with his good fortune. He gave a great feast to all his new neighbours and everyone was satisfied, except the fox.

"It is time I had my reward," said the fox to himself. "I'll sham illness and see how the prince will treat his old friend." So that is just what he did. He lay in the hall, groaning as loudly as he could.

"What a dreadful noise!" said everyone.

What do you think will happen now?

Here are the beginnings of two possible endings.
In your pair or group talk about how the story might finish in each case, and what might happen to the prince.

ENDING A
"He is a nuisance," said the prince. "Get rid of him someone. Throw him on the dung hill . . ."

ENDING B
"Quiet!" shouted the prince. "This is my dear friend and he must be given the best of everything . . ."

This is how the writer did finish the story:

"He is a nuisance," said the prince. "Get rid of him, someone. Throw him on the dung-hill."

There the poor beast lay with not a friend in all the world. One day Prince Csihan passed that way. "Hey, Prince of Nettles!" howled the fox. "A fine prince you have turned out. Have you ground much flour lately?"

"Hush!" said the prince. "Someone will hear you."

"Prince Miller!" bawled the fox. "There may be honour among princes and foxes, but none among millers."

"Be quiet, and you shall be my best friend and companion." And he took the fox in, and from that day fox and prince sat at the same table and ate the same food.

So they lived happily, and I dare say there are doing so still, if they are not dead.

Prince of Nettles

After the miller's son has helped the fox to hide, he is very richly rewarded. When later in the story he treats the fox very ungratefully he is not punished at all — unlike the unkind girls in the stories, *Two Sisters and Two Bowls* **and** *How Crab Got Its Back.*

Is this because —

1. Boys aren't expected to behave kindly towards others.

2. Boys aren't expected to look after others in need of help such as the old and sick.

3. It's more important for boys to win riches and status through their own efforts (fair or unfair) than to be given them.

4. It's more important for girls to learn to behave in a kindly and caring way than boys.

5. It's more important that girls should learn to 'behave properly' than boys.

6. 'Behaving properly' means something different when applied to boys and girls.

WHAT DO YOU THINK?

Talk about the statements above and try to say what you think.

To get your discussion started, divide the statements into those you AGREE with and those you DISAGREE with.

Heroes & Heroines

HEROINES

Remember what Alison Lurie said about heroines in the traditional fairy stories and folk tales that we are most familiar with:

'Things just happen to them: they are persecuted by wicked stepmothers, eaten by wolves, or fall asleep for a hundred years. All most of them ever seem to do is wait patiently for the right prince to come, or for someone else to rescue them from dangers and enchantments. . .

HEROES

Heroes also had their set ways of behaving: they had to be handsome, brave, never feel any doubts, and willing to kill dragons, giants and other men without a moment's hesitation or thought. Perhaps people should also worry about ideas readers of fairy tales might get about what boys are supposed to be — handsome and active and violent and thoughtless.

PROPER BEHAVIOUR: YESTERDAY

Read through the following list of words and phrases and decide which you think describe the traditional heroine, and which describe the traditional hero. Write your decisions on to the top part of a chart, like the one on the next page headed YESTERDAY'S HEROINE and YESTERDAY'S HERO. (You will need to draw a bigger chart, of course!)

ACTIVE   HANDSOME   LOVING   RESOURCEFUL   HELPLESS

INDEPENDENT   BOLD   QUIET   GOOD MANNERED   KIND

OBEDIENT   HONEST   LOYAL   BRAVE   DAINTY   BEAUTIFUL

GENTLE   PATIENT   CARING   FORCEFUL   DETERMINED

ADVENTUROUS   GRACEFUL   COMMANDING   VULNERABLE

SWEET TEMPERED   HONOURABLE   CONFIDENT   CHIVALROUS

GOOD AT FIGHTING   GOOD AT SEWING   INTELLIGENT   TIMID

PROPER BEHAVIOUR: TODAY

If a modern fairy story or folk tale was being written that showed children — both girls **and** boys — how to 'behave properly', what kinds of behaviour do you think could be encouraged?

Would it be different for boys and girls?

Make a list of qualities and ways of behaving that you think might be encouraged today in a modern fairy story or folk tale. Write your lists on to the bottom part of the chart headed TODAY'S HEROINE AND HERO.

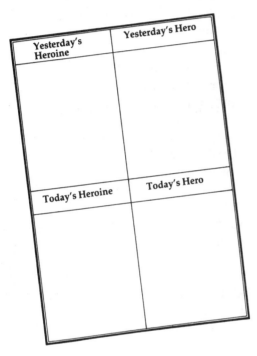

Here are some ideas to start you off:

Firstly go through your lists for YESTERDAY'S HEROINE AND HERO. Are there any qualities or ways of behaving that you think are still worth encouraging? Write them on to the chart. You could apply them to either girls or boys or to both.

Add to the lists. These are a few suggestions:

ABLE TO LOOK AFTER YOURSELF SENSITIVE   HAVING A SENSE OF HUMOUR   GENEROUS   STRONG POLITE   SELF-RELIANT...

Remember you can write the same things for girls **and** boys if you want to.

COMPARISONS

When you have finished, compare your lists with others in the class and talk about your decisions.

Are any of the lists the same for TODAY'S heroes (boys) and heroines (girls)?

If there are differences, what are they? Why are there differences?

Compare YESTERDAY'S and TODAY'S heroines and YESTERDAY'S and TODAY'S heroes.

Who has changed more?

Should there be changes in both heroines and heroes?

To Read or Not to Read

It has been said by some people that modern children shouldn't read fairy tales because they will get the idea that girls are supposed to be beautiful and good and helpless and dull, and that boys are meant to be handsome and active and violent and thoughtless.

WHAT DO YOU THINK?

Discuss the following statements about the way heroines and heroes are presented in fairy or folk stories. Decide which statements you agree with. Then in a few lines write down your opinion.

1. Fairy stories should be re-written with modern heroes and heroines for modern children.

2. It's not worth worrying about; children don't take much notice of what happens in stories.

3. All traditional fairy and folk stories should be banned from bookshops and libraries.

4. Parents and teachers should read fairy and folk stories first and decide whether or not they are suitable for children.

5. Children should be encouraged to read and understand fairy stories and folk tales.

6. Everyone knows that what happens in stories and what happens in real life are different.

4. DOING IT NATURALLY

Gone is Gone
The Man Who Knew Better
The Husband Who Stayed at Home

Gone is Gone

In the north country, where grass grows on the roofs of the cottages, there once lived a farmer who was not pleased with his lot in life. "I do more work in a day than you do in three," he said to his wife almost every noon-time and evening when he came in from the fields. "I toil and sweat, ploughing and sowing and harvesting, while you laze around the house."

At last his wife grew tired of hearing this talk. "Very well, husband," she said. "Tomorrow I will do your work, and you can do mine. I'll go out to cut the hay, and you can stay here and keep the house." "Good," the husband said, and he laughed to himself, thinking how easy it would be.

So the next morning the wife put the scythe over her shoulder and went out into the fields. Her husband thought he would begin by churning the cream, so there would be butter for the porridge at dinner. He churned and he churned, yet the butter did not come. "This is hot work," he said, and he went out the cottage door and down into the cellar to get some ale.

But just as he turned the tap on the barrel, he heard a noise overhead, which was the pig coming into the cottage, because he had left the door open. He ran up the cellar steps as fast as he could, but he was too late. The pig had already knocked over the churn, and was rooting and grunting in it. The husband shouted and ran at the pig, and booted him out the door. Then he turned and looked at the churn lying on its side with the cream spilt over the floor.

"Well," he said. "Gone is gone."

Then he remembered the ale, and ran back down to the cellar. But he had left the tap open, and all the ale had run out of the barrel, so that there was none left to drink.

"Well, gone is gone," he said again.

Now the husband thought he would grind some oatmeal for the porridge. But while he was doing this he heard the cow mooing in the barn, and remembered that she was still shut up in her stall and had had nothing to eat all morning. As he hurried to let her out, he saw that the sun was already high in the sky. He thought that it was too late and too far to lead the cow down to the meadow, and that instead he would cut her some grass from the cottage roof, for a fine crop was growing there.

Then he said to himself that it would be much easier if he could only get the cow herself onto the roof. So he laid a plank across from the hill at the back of the cottage, and fetched her out of her stall. She didn't want to go onto the roof very much; but he pulled and coaxed and at last he got her over. Then he thought he had better tie her up, so she wouldn't fall off. So he fastened a rope to her halter, and out the other end down the chimney.

He climbed down off the roof and hurried back into the cottage. It was full of chickens, for he had left the door open again, and they had got into the oats. He shouted and ran at the chickens and shooed them out the door. Then he turned and looked at the bowl knocked over, and all the oatmeal that he had ground scattered over the floor.

"Well," he said. "Gone is gone."

He took the end of the cow's rope that was hanging down the chimney and tied it around his leg. Then he filled the big iron kettle with water and hung it over the fire, for it was dinner-time; and as fast as he could he ground more oats. The water began to boil, and he put them in. But while he was doing this, the cow fell off the roof, and as she fell she dragged the husband up the chimney by his leg. There he stuck fast, shouting and cursing; and as for the cow, she hung halfway down the wall outside.

It was now long past noon, and the wife, who had been cutting hay all morning, grew tired of waiting for her husband to call her home to dinner and started back to the cottage. As she came up the hill the first thing she saw was the cow hanging from the roof. She ran up and cut the rope with her scythe, and the cow fell to the ground. At the same time, inside, down fell her husband headfirst into the kettle of porridge.

The wife heard the noise and ran into the cottage. There was spilt cream and oats everywhere, and a smell of ale from the cellar, and her husband upside down in the kettle. She pulled him out, and there he stood on the floor dripping porridge.

"Well, husband," said she, "Gone is gone. From today forth, you do your work, and I'll do mine, and we'll say no more about it."

The Man
Who Knew Better

Once upon a time there was a man who thought his wife did nothing right in the house. He thought she did *this* wrong, and *that* wrong, and that *this* could be different, and *that* could be better. So at last, one evening, when he came in from work, and began grumbling and shouting the same as usual, she said, "Don't always be cross, my dear. We'll change our work, you and I. You shall do my work, and I'll do yours. Then you can show me how it ought to be."

The man thought it was a fine idea. So the next morning, the woman went to work in the fields with a scythe over her shoulder. And the man stayed at home to keep house.

Well, he just lay about for a time, just did nothing but scratch himself and snooze a bit and talk to the flies crawling up the wall. He thought it was an easy job keeping house.

Then, as time was getting on, he decided he'd have to get busy if dinner was to be ready. So he thought he'd churn the butter first.

They'd need butter for dinner.

But when he'd churned for a few minutes, he felt thirsty, and thought he'd go down to the cellar for a mug of ale. Well, he went down to the cellar, and he'd just set the tap running down there, when he heard the pig come snuffling into the kitchen over his head, for he'd left all the doors open, you see. So he left the tap running with ale and dashed up the cellar steps, thinking the pig would be sure to upset the churn.

When he got into the kitchen, the pig *had* upset the churn, and was standing grunting and snuffling in among the pools of cream, making slippery cream pats wherever he moved his hooves. And of course the man slipped and slithered on those cream pats, and got more and more angry, and yelled and shouted, and managed to give the pig a terrific kick which landed it flat on the floor.

Then he suddenly remembered the tap. He dashed down the steps again, two at a time, but when he got into the cellar, every drop of ale had run out of the barrel, through the tap, and all over the cellar floor.

"Well, that's the end of that," he said, giving the empty barrel a kick. "I'll fill the churn with cream again, and have another go at making the butter."

But he'd no sooner started to make the butter again when he remembered he hadn't let the cow out of the byre. She'd been shut up there since yesterday and hadn't had a bite to eat or a drop to drink all morning. So he rushed round to the byre to let her out.

He was just going to take her to the meadow — for that was her usual place, the meadow — when he suddenly remembered how late it was getting. "It's nearly dinner-time," he said to himself. "I haven't time to take her up there. She'll have to go up on the roof and make the best of it." For in the country where he lived, you see, the roofs were all thatched, and there was grass growing there. But how could he get her up on the roof, that was the question? Well, luckily the house was built against a bit of a hill, and he reckoned that if he could get hold of a plank, he could lay it from the hill up to the roof, and get the cow to walk along it.

He thought he knew where there was a plank that would do nicely. But he couldn't leave the churn in the kitchen, because the baby was crawling all over the floor and was bound to upset it; she never left anything alone, that one. The only thing he could think of to do about this, was to pick up the churn, all full of cream, and put it on his back, and he staggered out like this.

Then he suddenly thought the cow still hadn't had a drink. She certainly wouldn't find anything to drink up on the roof, so he'd better give her a drink before he got her up there. He bent down to get some water out of the well, but when he did, the churn on his back tilted and all the cream ran into his neck and his ears and his hair and dripped down into the well.

Well, after that he was feeling tired, although he hadn't got very much done. But he managed to get the cow up on the roof. Now it was nearly dinner-time and he hadn't got anything ready. He decided he'd leave everything and just make some porridge. He filled the pot with water and put it on the fire. But then he suddenly thought, "Suppose the cow falls off the roof while I'm in the kitchen." So he hunted for a rope, and rushed outside, and climbed as fast as he could to the roof. The cow was still there.

First he tied the rope round her neck. But she didn't like it, so he tied it round her leg. Then he wondered where to tie the other end. At last he had a really clever idea. He dropped the rope down the chimney, climbed down from the roof again, nipped into the kitchen, picked up the end of the rope that had come down the chimney and tied it round his leg.

By now, the water in the porridge pot was boiling away, but he hadn't got any porridge meal ready, and it was nearly dinner-time. He ran to get the porridge meal, and just then the cow *did* fall off the roof. She only fell half-way because the rope stopped her. There she stayed, swinging in the air half-way down the wall. And the rope pulled the man by his leg half-way up the chimney, and there he stuck. Now it was dinner-time.

All this while the woman had been working hard in the field, thinking how nice it would be to come home to a dinner that someone else had cooked for her — everything ready on the table, steaming hot, and something cool and refreshing to drink. What a change that would be! But the time seemed to be a long while coming. The day went on, the sun crossed the sky, and still her husband hadn't called her. She got tired of waiting, and decided to go home.

When she got near the house she saw the poor old cow hanging half-way down the wall. "Lawks a mercy!" she cried. She ran to the cow as fast as she could with her big scythe bumping and jabbing into her shoulder, and she took her scythe and cut through the rope, and down came the cow the rest of the way. But when she did this, the rope raced back through the chimney, and the man at the other end of it came down with a crumpled crash. The woman, of course, knew nothing about this. Only when she came into the kitchen, dearly hoping her dinner was ready, there he was standing on his head in the porridge pot!

The Husband Who Stayed at Home

Once upon a time there was a man so cross and bad-tempered that he thought his wife never did anything right in the house.

So one evening during the haymaking time, when he came home scolding and complaining, his wife said, "You think you could do the work of the house better than I?"

"Yes, I do," growled the husband. "Any ninny could!"

"Well, then, tomorrow let's switch our tasks. I'll go with the mowers and mow the hay. You stay here and do the housework."

The husband agreed at once. He thought it a very good idea.

Early the next morning his wife took a scythe over her shoulder and went out to the hayfield with the mowers; the man stayed in the house to do the work at home.

He decided first to churn the butter for their dinner. After he had churned a while, he became thirsty; he went down to the cellar to tap a pitcher of ale. He had just taken the bung out of the ale barrel and was about to put in the tap when overhead he heard the pig coming into the kitchen.

With the tap in his hand, he ran up the cellar steps as fast as he could, lest the pig upset the butter churn. When he came up to the kitchen, he saw that the pig had already knocked over the churn. The cream had run all over the floor and the pig was happily slurping it.

He became so wild with rage that he quite forgot the ale barrel in the cellar. He ran after the pig, slipped, and fell facedown into the cream.

When he scrambled to his feet, he caught the pig running through the door and gave it such a kick in the head that the pig dropped dead.

All at once he remembered the ale tap in his hand. But when he ran down to the cellar, every drop of ale had run out of the barrel.

There was no butter for their dinner, so he went into the dairy to look for more cream. Luckily there was enough cream left to fill the churn once more, and he again began to churn butter.

After he had thumped the churn for a while, he remembered that their milking cow was still shut up in the barn. The poor cow had had nothing to eat or drink all morning, and the sun was now high in the sky.

He had no time to take the cow down to the pasture, for the baby was crawling about in the spilt cream, and he still had to clean up the floor and the baby. He thought it would save time if he put the cow on the top of their house to graze. The flat roof of the house was thatched with sod, and a fine crop of grass was growing there.

Since the house lay close to a steep hill at the back, he thought that if he laid two planks across the thatched roof to the hill, he could easily get the cow up there to graze.

As he started out the door he realized he should not leave the churn in the kitchen with the baby crawling about. "The child is sure to upset it!" he thought.

So he lifted the churn onto his back and went out with it.

"I had best give the cow some water before I put her on the roof to graze," he said to himself. He took up a bucket to draw water from the well, but as he leaned over the well to fill the bucket, all the cream ran out of the churn, over his shoulder, and down into the well.

In a temper, he hurled the empty churn across the yard and went to water the cow. Then he searched for two planks to make a bridge from the hill to the roof of the house. After a great deal of trouble, he persuaded the cow to cross the planks onto the sod roof.

Now is was near dinnertime and the baby was crying. "I have no butter," he thought. "I'd best boil porridge."

So he hurried back to the kitchen, filled the pot with water, and hung it over the fire. Then he realized the cow was not tied; she could easily fall off the roof and break her legs.

Back he ran to the roof with a rope. Since there was no post to tie her to, he tied one end of the rope around the cow, and the other end he slipped down the hole in the roof that served as a chimney. When he came back to the kitchen he tied the loose end around his knee.

The water was now boiling in the pot, but the oatmeal still had to be ground for the porridge. He ground away and was just throwing the oatmeal into the pot when the cow fell off the roof.

As she fell, the rope on the man's knee jerked, and he was pulled up into the air. The pot of water was knocked over, putting the fire out, and the man dangled upside down above the hearth. Outside, the poor cow swung halfway down the house wall, unable to get up or down.

In the meantime, the wife had mowed seven lengths and seven breadths of the hayfield. She expected her husband to call her home to dinner. When he did not appear, she at last trudged off to their home.

When she got there, she saw the cow dangling in such a queer place that she ran up and cut the rope with her scythe. As soon as the rope was cut, the man fell down the hearth.

His wife rushed into the house to find her husband in the hearth, covered with ashes, the floor slippery with clots of cream and ground oatmeal, and the baby wailing.

When they had cleaned up the house and taken the cow out to pasture and hung up the pig for butchering, they sat down to eat stale bread without butter or porridge.

The wife said to him, "Tomorrow you'll get the right way of it."

"Tomorrow!" he spluttered. "You'll not be going out with the mowers tomorrow!"

"And why not? You agreed to it," said she. "Do you think the work of the house too hard?"

This the husband would not admit. "No indeed! If you can do it, I can do it!" he growled.

"Well, then!" said his wife.

They argued the rest of the day over who should mow and who should mind the house. There seemed no way to settle it until at last the husband agreed he would work in the fields three days a week and work in the house three days; his wife would take his place in the fields for three days, and take care of the house the other days.

With this compromise they lived quite peaceably, and neither the husband nor the wife complained very much at all.

Messages

Below is a list of the main differences between the three versions of the story. The first three sections, called the BEGINNING, the MIDDLE and the END, are about the characters and events in each story. The last two sections, called AUDIENCE and MESSAGE are not so easy. They tell you who the different stories might have been written for (the audience) and offer you ideas on the different messages each story has.

Using a chart like the one which follows, try to fit each description into the correct box.

The Beginning

- The husband is bad tempered and critical and his wife gets fed up with his complaints and challenges him to prove how easy housework really is.

- The husband is bad tempered and the wife seems to be very humble and asks to be shown how to do the housework better.

- The husband is a moaner but delighted to have an easy day at home when his wife offers it, fed up with him telling her she lazes around all day.

The Middle

- One version makes no mention of there being a baby to be looked after, the other two do.

- One version makes no mention of the churn on the man's back getting spilled.

- One version makes the man so angry he kills the pig.

The End

- The story ends without comment; we just discover what the wife finds when she returns home.

- The wife assumes he'll want to learn to do the housework better by practising the next day. She taunts him into wanting to prove the work isn't difficult and they end up sharing both jobs.

- The wife isn't cross but tells him they should each stick to their proper work.

Audience

- One story is aimed at very young children.

- One story is aimed at school pupils.

- One story is aimed at adult readers.

Message

- One story gives an example of a family where work and responsibility is shared.

- One story is mainly for fun and not to be taken too seriously.

- One story says that there is men's work and women's work and they should be kept separate.

	GONE IS GONE	THE MAN WHO KNEW BETTER	THE HUSBAND WHO STAYED AT HOME
Beginning			
Middle			
Ending			
Audience			
Message			

Gone is Gone, The Man Who Knew Better, The Husband Who Stayed at Home

Work in the home: What do you think?

The following statements are all to do with work in the home; what it's like and who does it. In your groups talk about the statements and decide which you agree with, which you disagree with, and those that you are not sure about. Be ready to give reasons for your decisions.

1. It's silly to share all the household jobs; people should do the things they're best at.

2. Women are naturally better at housework than men.

3. Work in the home is not very important.

4. It's not natural for women to work outside the home.

5. It's not natural for men to work in the home.

6. There isn't really that much work to do in the home.

7. Girls should do more housework than boys to prepare for when they have their own homes.

8. Work in the house demands a lot of effort.

9. Everyone who lives in the house should take responsibility for the housework.

10. Women shouldn't go out to work: it causes problems for their families.

11. Women have always done the household jobs — in every time and every place.

12. There is too much work in the house for one person to do alone.

13. Boys and men should do enough work in the home to avoid arguments.

14. It's not fair to expect a man who works all day to do work in the home.

After you have finished your discussion write your own views on working inside and outside the home.

Gone is Gone, The Man Who Knew Better, The Husband Who Stayed at Home

FOR WRITING

Write a story of your own, set in the present, in a city, where a man and a woman change places for a time.

Before you start writing think about the following:

— What are the characters of the man and the woman going to be like?

— What happens to make them decide to change places?

— What happens when they do?

— What kind of style is your story going to be written in?

— What kind of reader is your story aimed at? (very young? school age? adult?)

— What message does your story contain?

   For example does it say that changing places is possible? impossible? easy? difficult? stupid? worthwhile?

— What does your story say about the importance of housework?

5. READING THE CHANGES

The Lute Player
Gawain and Ragnell

The Lute Player

BEFORE READING

Here are four ingredients for you to include in a story. In your pair or group, talk about who the characters are, what the story might be about, and how it might go.

1. **A** and **B** are happily married. **A** is then captured and imprisoned by a far-off ruler.

2. **A** sends word to **B** to bring ransom money for **A's** rescue.

3. **B** thinks of a better plan. The rescue involves a disguise.

4. Things go wrong, but eventually everything ends happily.

AFTER READING

A lot of stories and fables end with the words, 'and the moral is. . .' and then the reader is told something about how people ought to behave, or what can be expected from life.

Here are some 'morals' that could end *The Lute Player*. Which do you think is the real message of the story?

1. Men are easily tricked.

2. Women make better judgements than men.

3. All wicked kings are soft-hearted underneath.

4. If women want adventures or success in life they have to pretend to be men.

5. Everyone should play a musical instrument.

6. Ministers aren't always the wisest in making decisions.

The Lute Player

Once upon a time a king and a queen lived quite happily in their small kingdom. The king held tournaments and practiced mock battles with his knights; but after a time he grew bored and restless. He longed to go out into the world to try his skill in battle, and to win fame and glory.

So he called his band of armed knights together and gave orders to start for a distant country where lived a cruel king who raided the countries all around him. The queen, who had always shared the duties of the kingdom, was now given full power to rule in his absence, He commanded his ministers to assist the queen in all things; then, taking tender leave of his wife, the king set out with his small force.

After a time the king reached the lands of the foreign ruler. He rode on until he came to a mountain pass where a large army lay in wait for him. His force was defeated; the king himself was taken prisoner.

He was carried off to the prison where the captives suffered badly. The prisoners were kept chained all night long, and in the morning they were yoked together like oxen to plough the land till it grew dark.

In the meantime the queen governed the land wisely and well. The country remained at peace with its neighbours and her subjects prospered. But when one year became two, and then three, the queen grieved at her husband's long absence. Since no word was received from him, she feared he had been killed.

When at last the poor king was able to send her a message, her grief turned to joy. The letter told of his capture and gave instructions for his rescue:

". . . Sell our castles and estates and borrow money to raise as large a fortune as you can. Either bring or send the gold to ransom me — for that is the only hope of deliverance from this terrible prison. . ."

The queen pondered the message. She was resolved to obtain his release as quickly as possible, but to raise so large a sum would take many months.

"Then if I bring the ransom gold myself," she thought, "this foreign king might seize the gold and imprison me, too. If I send messengers with the ransom, whom shall I trust? It is a long distance to travel with a cart full of gold! And what then if the ransom offer is refused or seized? This ruthless king may not want to ransom a prisoner — or he may be so wealthy he will laugh at our gold!"

The queen paced her chamber in despair. "If I do as the king requests, he would return home beggared and in debt, the country impoverished." These thoughts filled her mind until she was nearly distracted.

At last an idea came to her. She would journey to the distant land as a vagabond minstrel, a lute player, and she would rescue the king herself. She cut her long hair and dressed herself as a minstrel boy. Then she took her lute, and leaving word that she was going on a journey, she left the castle at night. She did not know if her bold plan would succeed; but she knew the ministers would be horrified and detain her if they could.

At first the queen rode alone, but soon she joined a party of pilgrims journeying her way. Later she joined a group of merchants and peddlers. The young minstrel who played the lute so well and sang so gaily was welcome company to the travellers.

In this way she neared her destination in little more than a month. Leaving the party of merchants, she headed for the steep mountain pass and the country where her husband was imprisoned. She had become thin and browned by the sun, and the bright colours of her minstrel cloak were dusty and worn.

When at last she arrived at the palace of the foreign king, she walked all around it and at the back she saw the prison. Then she went into the great court in front of the palace. Taking her lute in her hands, she began to play so artfully that all who heard her felt as though they could never hear enough.

After she had played for some time she began to sing, and her voice was sweeter than the nightingale's:

> *I come from my own country far*
> *Into this foreign land;*
> *Of all I own, I take alone*
> *My sweet lute in my hand.*
>
> *Oh, who will thank me for my song*
> *Reward my simple lay?*   A lay is a ballad or song
> *Like lover's sighs it still shall rise*
> *To greet thee day by day.*
>
> *My song begs for your pity*
> *And gifts from out your store;*
> *And as I play my gentle lay*
> *I linger near your door.*
>
> *And if you hear my singing*
> *Within your palace, sire,*
> *Oh, give I pray, this happy day,*
> *To me my heart's desire.*

No sooner had the king heard this touching song, sung by such a lovely voice, than he had the singer brought before him.

"Welcome, lute player," said he. "Where do you come from?"

"My country, sire, is far away across many lands. I wander from country to country, and I earn my living with my music."

"Stay here then a few days, and when you wish to leave, I will give you as reward what you ask for in your song — your heart's desire."

So the lute player stayed on in the palace and played and sang songs both merry and sad. The king, who was charmed and beguiled by the songs and the music, never tired of listening and almost forgot to eat or drink.

After three days the lute player came to take leave of the king.

"Well," said the king, "what do you desire as your reward?"

"Sire, give me one of your prisoners. You have so many in your prison, and I should be glad of a companion on my journeys. When I hear his happy voice as I travel along, I shall think of you and thank you."

"Come along then," said the king, "choose whomever you wish." And he took the lute player through the prison himself.

The queen walked about among the prisoners, and at length she picked out her husband and took him with her on her journey home. Again they travelled the roads with parties of pilgrims and traders, and the king never suspected that the thin, sunbrowned minstrel who entertained the travellers could be his queen.

At last they reached the border of their own country. "Let me go now, kind lad," said her companion. "I am no common prisoner but the king of this country. Let me go free and ask what you will as your reward."

"Do not speak of reward," answered the lute player. "Go in peace."

"Then come with me, friend, and be my guest."

"When the proper time comes I shall be at your palace," said the minstrel, and so they parted.

The queen took a shorter way home, arriving at the castle before the king. She changed her clothes, putting on her most splendid gown and a high silk headdress.

An hour later, all the people in the castle were running to the courtyard crying, "Our king has come back! After three long years, our king has returned!"

The king greeted everyone kindly, but to his queen he said reproachfully, "Did you not receive my message? I laid a long time in prison waiting to be ransomed! Now you greet me lovingly, but it was a young lute player who rescued me and brought me home!"

The queen had expected to tell the king in the privacy of their chamber the reasons for her disguise and perilous journey, for she feared he would be angry that she had not sent the ransom money. But before she could make a suitable reply, a spiteful minister standing nearby said, "Sire, when news of your imprisonment arrived, the queen left the castle and only returned today."

At this the king looked stricken and sorrowful. He turned away to confer with his ministers, for he thought the queen had deserted him in his time of need. The queen returned to her chamber and put on again her travel-stained minstrel cloak and hood. Taking her lute, she slipped down to the castle courtyard where she sang in a sweet clear voice, the verses she had sung in a far off land:

> I sing the captive's longing
> Within his prison wall,
> Of hearts that sigh when none are nigh
> To answer to their call.

And if you hear my singing
Within your palace, sire,
Oh give, I pray, this happy day,
To me my heart's desire.

As soon as the king heard this song he ran out to meet the lute player, took him by the hand, and led him into the castle.

"Here," he cried, is the boy who released me from my prison. And now, my true friend, I will indeed give you your heart's desire."

"I ask only your trust and love," said she, throwing off the hooded cloak and revealing herself as the queen. "And I beg that you listen to my story."

A cry of astonishment rang through the hall. The king stood amazed, then rushed to embrace her.

"My dear husband," said the queen as she led him to one side, "I did receive your message, but I chose to follow another plan." Then the queen told him all that had troubled her about the ransom plan, and why she thought it the wiser course to rescue the king, instead, through her skill as a lute player.

"Thus," she ended, "you return not to a sorry kingdom of debts and people overburdened with taxes, but to a prosperous land and contented subjects."

Then the king rejoiced in the wisdom and courage of the queen and, in gratitude, proclaimed a seven day feast of celebration throughout the land.

Gawain & Ragnell

BEFORE READING

Before you read the last story in this collection see if you can do some guessing about it.

Questions

Work out the answers to these questions:

1. What is it that women desire above all else?
    You can have up to 5 guesses at this.

2. A woman is changed by magic into a hideous shape as a punishment for upsetting her stepbrother. Decide which of the following are the most likely reasons for this action:

    - for refusing to marry someone chosen by her brother
    - for being bold and unwomanly
    - for stealing his most precious possession
    - for being more loved by their mother than he was
    - for singing out of tune.

3. A man is offered the choice of having his wife extremely ugly **either** by day **or** by night, and beautiful the rest of the time. What would you advise him to decide?

Themes

These are the four themes in the story:

- A woman's right to choose
- An evil enchantment needing courage to be broken
- Romance and marriage
- Great loyalty needed by main character

Here are four well known tales — each involve at least one of the above.
Match them up, and add any more stories you can think of.

> *The Frog Prince*
> *Beauty and the Beast*
> *Cinderella*
> *Rapunzel*

Qualities

The main character has these four **qualities**. Which do you think will be the **most important?** Which do you think will be the **least important?**

1. bravery in battle
2. understanding the feelings of others
3. courtesy and politeness
4. loyalty to the King.

Gawain and The Lady Ragnell

Long ago, in the days of King Arthur, the finest knight in all Britain was the king's nephew Gawain. He was, by reputation, the bravest in battle, the wisest, the most courteous, the most compassionate, and the most loyal to his king.

One day in late summer, Gawain was with Arthur and the knights of the court at Carlisle in the north. The King returned from the day's hunting looking so pale and shaken that Gawain followed him at once to his chamber.

"What has happened, my lord?" asked Gawain with concern.

Arthur sat down heavily. "I had a very strange encounter in Inglewood forest . . . I hardly know what to make of it." And he related to Gawain what had occurred.

"Today I hunted a great white stag," said Arthur. "The stag at last escaped me and I was alone, some distance from my men. Suddenly a tall, powerful man appeared before me with sword upraised."

"And you were unarmed?"

"Yes. I had only my bow and a dagger in my belt. He threatened to kill me," Arthur went on. "And he swung his sword as though he meant to cut me down on the spot! Then he laughed horribly and said he would give me one chance to save my life."

"Who was this man?" cried Gawain. "Why should he want to kill you?"

"He said his name was Sir Gromer, and he sought revenge for the loss of his northern lands .

"A chieftain from the north!" exclaimed Gawain. "But what is this one chance he spoke of?"

"I gave him my word I would meet him one year from today, unarmed, at the same spot, with the answer to a question!" said Arthur.

Gawain started to laugh, but stopped at once when he saw Arthur's face. "A question! Is it a riddle? And one year to find the answer? That should not be hard!"

"If I can bring him the true answer to the question, 'What is it that women most desire, above all else?' my life will be spared." Arthur scowled. "He is sure I will fail. It must be a foolish riddle that no one can answer."

"My lord, we have one year to search the kingdom for answers," said Gawain confidently. "I will help you. Surely one of the answers will be the right one."

"No doubt you are right — someone will know the answer." Arthur looked more cheerful. "The man is mad, but a chieftain will keep his word."

For the next twelve months, Arthur and Gawain asked the question from one corner of the kingdom to the other. Then at last the appointed day drew near. Although they had many answers, Authur was worried.

"With so many answers to choose from, how do we know which is the right one?" he asked in despair. "Not one of them has the ring of truth."

A few days before he was to meet Sir Gromer, Arthur rode out alone through the golden gorse and purple heather. The track led upward toward a grove of great oaks. Arthur, deep in thought, did not look up until he reached the edge of the oak wood. When he raised his head, he pulled up suddenly in astonishment.

Before him was a grotesque woman. She was almost as wide as she was high, her skin was mottled green, and spikes of weedlike hair covered her head. Her face seemed more animal than human.

The woman's eyes met Arthur's fearlessly. "You are Arthur the king," she said in a harsh, croaking voice. "In two days time you must meet Sir Gromer with the answer to a question."

Arthur turned cold with fear. He stammered. "Yes . . . yes . . . that is true. Who are you? How did you know of this?"

"I am the lady Ragnell. Sir Gromer is my stepbrother. You haven't found the true answer, have you?"

"I have many answers," Arthur replied curtly. "I do not see how my business concerns you." He gathered up the reins, eager to be gone.

"You do not have the right answer." Her certainty filled him with a sense of doom. The harsh voice went on, "But I know the answer to Sir Gromer's question."

Arthur turned back in hope and disbelief. "You do? Tell me the true answer to his question, and I will give you a large bag of gold."

"I have no use for gold," she said coldly.

"Nonsense, my good woman. With gold you can buy anything you want!" He hestitated a moment, for the huge grotesque face with the cool, steady eyes unnerved him. He went on hurriedly, "What is it you want? Jewelry? Land? Whatever you want I will pay you — that is, if you truly have the right answer."

"I know the answer. I promise you that!" She paused. "What I demand in return is that the knight Gawain become my husband."

There was a moment of shocked silence. Then Arthur cried, "Impossible! You ask the impossible, woman!"

She shrugged and turned to leave.

"Wait, wait a moment!" Rage and panic overwhelmed him, but he tried to speak reasonably.

"I offer you gold, land, jewels. I cannot give you my nephew. He is his own man. He is not mine to give!"

"I did not ask you to *give* me the knight Gawain," she rebuked him. "If Gawain himself agrees to marry me, I will give you the answer. Those are my terms."

"Impossible!" he spluttered. "I could not bring him such a proposal."

"If you should change your mind, I will be here tomorrow", said she, and disappeared into the oak woods.

Shaken from the weird encounter, Arthur rode homeward at a slow pace.

"Save my own life at Gawain's expense? Never!" he thought. "Loathsome woman! I could not even speak of it to Gawain."

But the afternoon air was soft and sweet with birdsong, and the fateful meeting with Sir Gromer weighed on him heavily. He was torn by the terrible choice facing him.

Gawain rode out from the castle to meet the king. Seeing Arthur's pale, strained face, he exclaimed, "My lord! Are you ill? What has happened?"

"Nothing . . . nothing at all." But he could not keep silent long. "The colossal impudence of the woman! A monster, that's what she is! That creature, daring to give me terms!"

"Calm yourself, uncle," Gawain said patiently. "What woman? Terms for what?"

Arthur sighed. "She knows the answer to the question. I didn't intend to tell you."

"Why not? Surely that's good news! What is the answer?"

"She will not tell me until her terms are met," said the king heavily. "But I assure you, I refuse to consider her proposal!"

Gawain smiled. "You talk in riddles yourself, uncle. Who is this woman who claims to know the answer? What is her proposal?"

Seeing Gawain's smiling, expectant face, Arthur at first could not speak. Then, with eyes averted, the king told Gawain the whole story, leaving out no detail.

"The lady Ragnell is Sir Gromer's stepsister? Yes, I think she would know the right answer," Gawain said thoughtfully. "How fortunate that I will be able to save your life!"

"No! I will not let you sacrifice yourself!" Arthur cried.

"It is my choice and my decision," Gawain answered. "I will return with you tomorrow and agree to the marriage — on condition that the answer she supplies is the right one to save your life."

Early the following day, Gawain rode out with Arthur. But not even meeting the loathsome lady face to face could shake his resolve. Her proposal was accepted.

Gawain bowed courteously. "If on the morrow your answer saves the king's life, we will be wed."

On the fateful morning, Gawain watched the king stow a parchment in his saddlebag. "I'll try all these answers first," said Arthur.

They rode together for the first part of the journey. Then Arthur, unarmed as agreed, rode on alone to Inglewood to meet Sir Gromer.

The tall, powerful chieftain was waiting, his broadsword glinting in the sun.

Arthur read off one answer, then another, and another. Sir Gromer shook his head in satisfaction.

"No, you have not the right answer!" he said raising his scord high. "You've failed, and now . . ."

"Wait! Arthur cried. "I have one more answer. What a woman desires above all else is the power of sovereignty — the right to exercise her own will."

With a loud oath the man dropped his sword. "You did not find that answer by yourself!" he shouted. "My cursed stepsister, Ragnell, gave it to you. Bold, interfering hussy! I'll run her through with my sword . . . I'll lop off her head . . ." Turning, he plunged into the forest, a string of horrible curses echoing behind him.

Arthur rode back to where Gawain waited with the monstrous Ragnell. They returned to the castle in silence. Only the grotesque Lady Ragnell seemed in good spirits.

The news spread quickly throughout the castle. Gawain, the finest knight in the land, was to marry this monstrous creature! Some tittered and laughed at the spectacle; others said the lady Ragnell must posses very great lands and estates; but mostly there was stunned silence.

Arthur took his nephew aside nervously. "Must you go through with it at once? A postponement perhaps?"

Gawain looked at him steadily. "I gave my promise, my lord. The lady Ragnell's answer saved your life. Would you have me . . ."

"Your loyalty makes me ashamed! Of course you cannot break your word." And Arthur turned away.

The marriage took place in the abbey. Afterward, with Gawain and the lady Ragnell sitting at the high dias table beside the king and queen, the strange wedding feast began.

"She takes the space of two women on the chair," muttered the knight Gareth. "Poor Gawain!"

"I would not marry such a creature for all the land in Christendom!" answered his companion.

An uneasy silence settled on the hall. Only the monstrous Lady Ragnell displayed good spirits and good appetite. Throughout the long day and evening, Gawain remained pleasant and courteous. In no way did his manner toward his strange bride show other than kind attention.

The wedding feast drew to a close. Gawain and his bride were conducted to their chamber and were at last alone.

The lady Ragnell gazed at her husband thoughtfully.

"You have kept your promise well and faithfully," she observed.

Gawain inclined his head. "I could not do less, my lady."

"You've shown neither revulsion nor pity," she said. After a pause she went on, "Come now, we are wedded! I am waiting to be kissed."

Gawain went to her at once and kissed her. When he stepped back, there stood before him a slender young woman with gray eyes and a serene, smiling face.

His scalp tingled in shock. "What manner of sorcery is this?" he cried hoarsely.

"Do you prefer me in this form?" she smiled and turned slowly in a full circle.

But Gawain backed away warily. "I . . . yes . . . of course . . . but . . . I don't understand . . ." For this sudden evidence of sorcery, with its unknown powers, made him confused and uneasy.

"My stepbrother, Sir Gromer, has always hated me," said the lady Ragnell. "Unfortunately, through his mother, he has a knowledge of sorcery, and so he changed me into a monstrous creature. He said I must live in that shape until I could persuade the greatest knight in Britain to willingly choose me for his bride. He said it would be an impossible condition to meet!"

"Why did he hate you so cruelly?"

Her lips curled in amusement. "He thought me bold and unwomanly because I defied him. I refused his commands both for my property and my person."

Gawain said with admiration, "You won the 'impossible' condition he set, and now his evil spell is broken!"

"Only in part." Her clear gray eyes held his. "You have a choice, my dear Gawain, which way will I be. Would you have me in this, my own shape, at night and my former ugly shape by day? Or would you have me grotesque at night in our chamber, and my own shape in the castle by day? Think carefully before you choose."

Gawain was silent only a moment. He knelt before her and touched her hand.

"It is a choice I cannot make, my dear Ragnell. It concerns you. Whatever you choose to be — fair by day or fair by night — I will willingly abide by it."

Ragnell released a long, deep breath. The radiance in her face overwhelmed him.

"You have answered well, dearest Gawain, for your answer has broken Gromer's evil spell completely. The last condition he set has been met! For he said that if, after marriage to the greatest knight in Britain, my husband freely gave me the power of choice, the power to exercise my own will, the wicked enchantment would be broken forever."

Thus, in wonder and in joy, began the marriage of Gawain and the lady Ragnell.

Gawain & Ragnell

AFTER READING

'Thus, in wonder and in joy, began the marriage of Gawain and Lady Ragnell.'

But — (think of it) —

- What will Sir Gromer think of next now that he has lost?

- What will the courtiers think of Lady Ragnell's sudden change?

- What else will Lady Ragnell want to decide for herself?

- Will Gawain go off into battle again?

Write a second part of this tale, telling the story of what happens next to Gawain and Lady Ragnell. What was their marriage like? What further adventures did they have?

Your Own Story

Having read this booklet and discussed the stories and tales and perhaps having read more widely, you may like to choose one of the following suggestions to write about in a more extended way.

1. Take one of the stories you have written and improve on it by re-writing or adding to it. You could also do some illustrations. If a group of you did this it may be possible to publish your writing as a school anthology.

2. Look back at the section called 'See How They've Changed'. Write an essay that describes the sort of changes that have been made to two or three of the versions of *Little Red Riding Hood*. Use examples from each story to illustrate the points you make and explain why these changes have taken place.

3. In a group do a small survey amongst young children you know to find out which stories and tales they like best. Choose the most popular and write your own version. Read it to them and ask for their opinions. Write up the result of your survey in full.

4. Imagine you have been asked to introduce this booklet to another class who are just going to start work on it.

   Write down your views and opinions about the stories and the activities in the booklet and the way your class approached them. But remember not to give anything away about the stories themselves.

5. Find out from people at home what stories they were told when they were younger, and make a collection of these tales. Or choose just one to re-tell, presenting it so that it would appeal to a young reader.

6. Write a cartoon fairy story or folk tale. Don't try to draw pictures that have a lot of detail. Concentrate on the story line.

Further Reading

The following books contain fairy stories and folk tales that you might like to read on your own. The titles marked with an * contain stories and tales which break some of the conventions you have been used to.

1. *The Kingdom Under the Sea* Joan Aiken Puffin 0150 306 412

2. *'A Necklace of Raindrops' and Other Stories* Joan Aiken Puffin 01403 07540

3. *Tales from Grimm* U. Dolt and G. Summerfield WLE Storyworld Level 1 0796 239 474

4. *The Ivory City* Marcus Crouch Granada Dragon 0583 304 834

5. *'Auta the Giant Killer' and Other Nigerian Folk Stories* Kathleen Arnott OUP 0198 342 497

6. *Classic Fairy Tales* Hans Christian Anderson Gollancz 0575 021 888

7. *Fairy Tales* Terry Jones Pavilion Books Ltd 0907 516 033

8. * *'Clever Gretchen' and Other Forgotten Folk Tales* Alison Lurie Heinemann 0434 948 993

9. * *'The Practical Princess' and Other Liberating Fairy Tales* Jay Williams Hippo Scholastic 0590 721 704

10. *Caribbean Folk Tales and Legends* ed Andrew Salkey Bogle L'Ouverture Publications 0904 5211 76

11. *Listen to This Story* Grace Hallworth Methuen 0416 582 702

12. *The Whole World Storybook* Marcus Crouch Oxford 0192 781 030

13. *The Story Spirits* Annabel Williams Ellis Piccolo

14. * *'Tatterhood' and Other Tales* Ethel Johnston Phelps Feminist Press (Box 334 Old Westbury New York 11568)

15. * *The Maid of the North* Ethel Johnston Phelps Holt Rinehart and Winston 003 06 2374 X

16. *Three Solid Stones* Martha Mvungi African Writers Series Heinemann Ed Books 0435 901 591

Teachers' Notes

GENERAL

The activities in this booklet are based on the belief that children know a great deal about stories, their structure and conventions. While literary analysis is usually thought to be more appropriate to older students, our experience is that attention to the formal qualities of literature can be a rewarding experience for younger pupils without detracting from their enjoyment. Although it is hoped that the work offered here will be interspersed with stories that *are* simply to be read and enjoyed, the activities are based on the premise that literature is something to be thought about and talked about, and not just consumed. This kind of approach points forward to the kind of study that aims at developing students' understanding of the nature of texts and the societies which produced them, and in which they are read.

THE APPROACH

We have tried not to suggest a didactic approach to the stories in the presentation of the materials. By working through the activities presented in the booklet we hope pupils will be encouraged to explore and evaluate the messages of folk and fairy tales written in different places at different times, and to consider how children read and what they attend to.

GROUPINGS

Because of the booklet's emphasis on talk and collaboration, group and pair work is implied in most activities. However, the teacher will need to assess when particular groupings are most appropriate and when a whole class approach is required. This obviously will vary depending on the class, and will be influenced by different factors. In Section Two, 'See How They Change', for example, the reading demands made by the materials are high and many teachers will feel they need to plan a variety of approaches to the reading of the stories and activities to support slow readers in the class.

TIMING

The booklet could provide a continuous unit of work to be followed over, say, half a term. But obviously this is not the only approach. We suggest that early on teachers decide on the emphasis they want to give to the various sections. The experience of piloting the packs has indicated that it is worth extending the introductory activities suggested on page 4 headed 'Frogs and Princesses'. We suggest that reading a number of traditional tales with students, possibly giving over a lesson to individual or group reading of old favourites will provide a useful context for the work that follows. Then Sections One and Two are probably best worked through consecutively, as the work in 'What You Expect' provides a basis for the discussion of changes in re-telling and re-writing stories in Section Two. But how teachers organise the work will depend on the class and the particular 'slot' this unit occupies, and on the outcomes they wish to pursue. However, it is certainly something that needs advance planning.

On the activity pages there are a number of charts to be filled in by students. Teachers may want to save lesson time by drawing out and duplicating enlarged versions of the charts. For examples see pages 13 and 74.

Printed in Great Britain by Polestar Scientifica Ltd, Exeter